A BURFORD BOY

Robert Harvey Pearman
1916–1994

SUE SHAYLER

First Published in 2007

Published by Sue Shayler 2007

© Sue Shayler

ISBN 978-0-9555876-0-3

This book is dedicated to all who served in Bomber Command.

PREFACE

My father, with some reluctance, recalled memories of his time during World War 2, as a bomber pilot. With encouragement we talked and wrote them down. This is his straightforward and personal account.

He was a quiet, dignified man, a wonderful father and grandfather and I felt it important to have a record of his life, not only to hand down to future generations of our family, but also for others interested in our nation's history and the sacrifices made by Bomber Command – an understated service.

My mother's brief account at the end of the book, outlines the pressures and supporting role of a young wife and mother through the war years.

Sue

FOREWORD

The house, of flint and brick, has after thoughts of out-buildings in the dusty butter cream of Cotswold stone. The lounge is slightly dishevelled, as if taken by surprise at an unexpected visit. A pair of Jack Russells toast their strawberry pink bellies before the fire. The door flies open; two children erupt into the room. Floor boards vibrate briefly and the framed colour print of a Handley page Hampden trembles on its hook. Above this familiar Frank Wooton print hangs a bright metal D ring with its length of braided cable, the rip cord of a parachute. For Bob Pearman, sitting in the deep armchair, stroking the milk chocolate fur of a yellow eyed Burmese cat is a member, twice over, of the Caterpillar Club. Entry is involuntary and necessity only. As a caterpillar hangs by a silken thread, so members of the Club, which bears the same generic name, have saved their lives by hanging from silken cords beneath a silken canopy to float slowly down from their stricken aircraft to a safer, if less premeditated landing.

In November 1940, a Hampden, P.2079 of No.144 Squadron, was returning from a sortie to Munich, to its base at Hemswell. After nine hours in the air, fuel was running short. Never the easiest aircraft to fly on one engine, with small twin rudders at the end of a long tail boom; with a tired pilot and a tired crew in the darkness of a winter night, the spluttering and backfiring as the port engine drained the tanks was a signal to leave. The gunner, then the wireless operator slid out of the lower hatch at the base of the keep narrow fuselage. 'Ready, Skipper?' the navigator/ second pilot's voice proclaimed his anxiety to be off. A vortex of paper and maps fluttered up into the cockpit as the lower hatch was opened. Back with the pilot's canopy; unplug the intercom; check that the oxygen tube was free, then off with the Sutton harness. Twelve hundred feet on the altimeter, immersed in a sea of darkness, the slipstream snatched at his body as Sergeant Pearman went over the side. He brushed across the top of the wing as the doomed aircraft disappeared, a fleeting shadow in the enveloping night. There was a soft thudding noise above as the parachute lines jerked taut. The wind died to a steady updraught. A sense of inordinate relief suffused his mind and tired body; he felt as if all the tense anxieties and troubles were past as he hung, apparently motionless in the blackness about him. It was almost a surprise as the ground leapt up and he collapsed on his knees in the wet grass, then staggered to his feet to strike the quick release box and shed the harness of his silken support. A few miles away, P.2079 was transformed into five tons of torn and twisted metal, as empty, it thudded into the ground ...

A Revelation – Handley Page's Flying Suitcase by Rupert Cooling
(Air Enthusiast March 1981)

My thanks to those who encouraged and supported the gathering of this account.

Rupert 'Tiny' Cooling, fellow pilot and lifelong friend for his experience and guidance. Virginia Wootton, Michael Turner and 44 Squadron for permission to use the Hampden prints.

Chapter one

Bob's Story

Bob aged 5 years

I was born in 1916 in Burford. I lived with my mother Eliza, and brother John, in a house called Hill View in the High Street. My father, a farmer, died at the age of 33 years and my mother brought us up on her own. My memories of Burford go back to when it was an active village full of life, full of trades and full of skills. Richards was a tinsmith; he would make or repair kettles. Soden and Howse were both blacksmiths. David Francis was a wheelwright and undertaker. Bond had a bell foundry. Bowle was a saddler. Garnes were the brewers. Jamie Wall lived in the high street, and he made rope. Evans was a gunsmith. Wiggins in Witney Street had a tan yard and Burford had its own Electric Light Company and made its own electricity. There was a printer named Packer. Burford Golf Course and Bury Barn now stand on ground that belonged to Tansley Farm.

Saturday, of course, was the busiest day of the week. All the villagers came in to Burford to do their shopping and it would be busy all afternoon and evening, especially around six o'clock when everyone would stand outside Hollis's shop to listen to the loudspeaker giving all the football results. Villagers came into Burford on their bicycles with lamps lit by oil or acetyline. I can remember distinctly seeing little piles of used acetyline powder where people emptied and refilled their

Bob *(right)* John *(left)*

lamps. The earliest recollection I have of Burford was being pushed down Burford High street in a pram to the bottom of the hill to where Albert Barrett lived. He was also in a pram and he pushed his finger towards me and I grabbed it and bit it.

I used to watch Soden shoeing horses and I shall never forget the smell of the hot shoes burning into the hooves. I also used to spend a lot of time with Charlie Howse, the other blacksmith, because he used to make us hoops and guides and I'd be down there day after day pumping the bellows and watching him working. The local vicar was called Canon Emryss. He had a hooked nose, so of course he was quickly nicknamed 'Spike'.

Bob *(right)* and Bertie

The first time I was introduced to any crime at all was at a garden fete held at the vicarage. During this fete I helped myself to some apples – somebody spotted me – and unfortunately my cousin Bertie from Fulbrook, resembling me closely, was blamed for this and punished forthwith. Eventually the vicar came to see my mother when the true culprit was revealed, and I had to go and apologise to the vicar. Meanwhile Bertie Gillett, the innocent victim, was sent on the seaside outing as a recompense for the punishment he had received. A wonderful treat.

As I got a bit older we spent all summer long down by the river. There were different gangs of lads and there was great competition in boat building. The first boat I built was constructed out of rubber tubes. We scrounged these from local garages, repaired them, then built the raft over the top of them for buoyancy. The competition with the other lads was such that we had all our tubes slashed, so we had to find some other means of construction. The next one was made out of oil drums. Again we scrounged these from garages and again built the raft over the top of them. This was quite satisfactory until someone sabotaged them and put a hole in each of the drums. The third one we made consisted of an old shaft from a cart, which we thought would make a good keel. We put ribs on this shaft wrapped it up in a big

Bob aged 11 years

tarpaulin and made it in the style of a canoe except that it was very very heavy. We put this in the river at Upton and came down the river to Burford bridge with the boat gradually filling up with water – we struggled on to Guildenford where we finally sank.

My shoes had also disappeared with the boat, and I finally retrieved these after several diving attempts, because I dare not go home without them. The next boat was a lot more ambitious. In our gang was Dennis Pether, whose father was a builder in Burford, and also a lad called Jocky Smith. We would go up to the builder's yard in the daytime and look out the useful bits of wood to make a punt. We would move this wood to the back doors and at night we would nip back and pull this wood from under the doors. Jocky Smith would be there on his bicycle and he'd take the planks down to his yard, cut them into the required lengths as quickly as possible, so that no-one would recognise the wood and this punt was a great success. These boats were all 'tested' at Castle's meadow waterfall – if one made it, then it was ok. My main swimming place was at Upton – nowadays not at all interesting, but then it was the most popular swimming place around. There was a pole across the river dividing the deep water from the shallow.

Another centre of activity in Burford was the icecream shop, owned by a Mr. Rooke. He ordered his ice from Oxford and this was sent on the Oxford bus. This ice was then packed around the custard cream type mixture, and then it was a case of winding a handle attempting to get this mixture to freeze. This amazing treat was a threepenny dish of icecream.

3

A halfpenny cornet was nice, a one penny cornet was great but the threepenny dish was just amazing. We had no pocket money and if we wanted anything from the icecream man we had to pinch, scrounge, borrow, or cadge the money from somewhere. Nothing was simply bought and paid for. There just wasn't the money.

Burford attracted shoppers from as far afield as Sherborne, Barrington, Windrush, Westwell, Swinbrook, Asthall, Shipton, and they all came to Burford for their main supplies. Five butchers, three bakers and numerous grocery stores made good livings in Burford. The butchers and bakers delivered their goods to the outlying villages. I used to drive with Tommy Taylor who delivered petrol and paraffin to all the villages around for Mr. Evans the ironmonger. They had an old Model T Ford and one day Tommy Taylor asked me if I 'd like to drive this, and I remember as I was coming up the hill at Sherborne I had to change gear which meant you had to put your foot on the clutch and hold it down which put the car into second gear, whilst I could barely see over the steering wheel. Most of the deliveries in the Burford area were done by pony and trap, and you became familiar with each pony, being asked to hold these animals still. Baker Smith's horse was well known for biting, so he was avoided. Mr. Titcombe, the other baker, had a donkey and a handcart. The horses were sometimes tied to the gas lamps, which lined the high street.

There were mounting blocks dotted about. There was one outside the Three Pigeons, which is now the Mermaid, one outside the Bull and one outside Doctor Cheatle's house.

Most of the Burford lads used to sing in the choir. Choir practice took place on a Saturday night and then we attended all the services on Sundays. Archie Barrett pumped the organ. The organ had to be pumped by hand until the lead weight moved down to a certain mark, and sometimes if the air became low the organ groaned. In the Vestry as the procession moved off the choirboys would slip into cupboards on the way out, and when the procession reached the choir stalls they would find they only had half the choir. One day somebody poured

Some of the members of the choir

4

some ink into Charlie Ruck's nice new hat and the vicar decided to boot everyone out of the choir and said he'd start again.

The vicar came to see my mother and told her that if her boys would like to apologise he would have them back in the choir, but my mother said no, he shouldn't have kicked them out in the first place. We were paid five shillings a quarter for singing in the choir, but deductions were made for bad behaviour, or for services and choir practices missed. We were lucky if we ended up with sixpence. With this money we went straight round to Kate's fish shop and had fish and chips. This fish and chip shop was the centre of entertainment on a Saturday night. It was absolutely filthy, but it was the only one and people had no choice, and it did a roaring trade. The cinema was next door to Kate's and we went on a Saturday afternoon for three pence. Every week they had a different film but it seemed that everyone was called Champions of the Prize Ring and they were extremely boring. They were all silent films that seemed never ending, and Tommy Taylor's wife played the piano through the films.

One or two of us were very keen on skating, and again we skated at Upton between the Priory and the river. This particular field is low lying and slightly below the river level, and if it hadn't flooded Skew Bishop and I would go and start a trickle of water from the river into this meadow. Within two days there would be a nice flood ready for the winter freezing. We took jam jars with candles in them and skated in the evenings. On a Sunday it would be very crowded. Jim Wyatt charged sixpence to go in to his field but we nipped through the Priory to avoid paying.

Chapter two

In 1929 a Scout group started, the 1st Burford Troop, and this was to change our lives. A detailed record of all our Scout activities is to be found in the museum in Burford and I include some excerpts from it.

The Beginning Sunday, July 7th
The Vicar had promised to collect half a dozen boys who were really keen to take on scouting; we were to meet on Sunday evening on the vicarage lawn. Sunday evening came round, and, instead of half a dozen, a large crowd of nearly 20 boys appeared. This enthusiasm was splendid, and the Scoutmaster sincerely hoped it would last. However it was impossible to deal with so many at first, so, after the idea of scouting had been briefly explained, 12 of the older boys were chosen and the rest were promised that their turn would come before long. The names of the original 12 were:
Fred Bayliss, Walter Bowl, David Cook, Horace Harrod, Jack Pearman, Bob Pearman, Dennis Pether, Walter Reilly, Tom Townsend, Leslie Wilsden, Gerald Yates, Tom Yeatman.

Wednesday evenings were fixed for scouting; and the first meeting was held on July 17th in the Church House. We got to work straight away on knots for the Tenderfoot test. For the rest of July we were busy at Tenderfoot work, with some scouting games mostly played out of doors.

The SM was away for the first three weeks of August. By the time he came back, several scouts were ready to pass their Tenderfoot test. When they had passed the test they got their uniforms, which are paid for by weekly subscriptions. Our troop colour is: Maroon with khaki shirt, shorts and stockings.

The troop was finally organised into three patrols: Otters, Swifts and Peewits.

We took it in turns to write up the Log.

Swimming (written by Bob Pearman)
One day in the summer Mr Heywood took the troop up bathing. First of all we sat on the bank, and Mr Heywood talked to us about life saving and artificial respiration. Then he let us get into the water and try it. Reilly, who was life saving Barrett, pulled him under water to the bank, and Barrett was submerged. But on coming to the surface he was all smiles. Then Mr Heywood put some aluminium plates in the water; we dived for them, but the water was so dirty that we could not see them; the SM got them out in the end. Some of them are still at the bottom of the river, I'm afraid. I think we enjoyed that evening very much.

Winter evenings
Scouting should be an outdoor activity, but chances of an afternoon in the country were few and there was not much point in going out on dark foggy evenings.

Here is an account of the kind of meeting the troop held on winter evenings:
The church clock, dimly seen in the lamplight points to a quarter to eight, and a rather chilly group of scouts is waiting outside the Church House until someone shall produce the key and let them in. The door is at last opened, and we swarm into the long room. The weekly subscriptions are collected amid a good deal of noise. 'Hi! The SM wants your subscriptions'. 'Oh sir, I've forgotten mine, may I pay next week?' 'How much have I got left?' 'May I have a new badge? I've lost mine' etc. etc.

At length the SM laden with coffers, signals Fall In and we have prayers. After prayers the troop is inspected for points for the Patrol competition. This patrol competition runs for two months, points being given for work, games, turnout etc. the winning patrol has the privilege of carrying the Union Jack and of falling in at the head of the troop.

Inspection over, the troop does some drill by signals, ending up with 'follow my leader' at the double, in and out of figure eights and spirals – quite warm work. Then the scouts sit round while there is instruction in some of the

Bob *(left)*

7

2nd class work, such as first aid. This part of the evening would go much better if everybody remembered to bring their note-books.

Next, a bit of rehearsing; our show is coming off before long, and we are getting busy on it, but this part of the work will be written up in the Log Book with the description of the show itself. Soon after 8.30 the patrols disperse to their own particular corners and do their own patrol work – not very hard work, I'm afraid, judging by the amount of noise they make. Then there is just time for a game; the most popular one is the hat game. Another is 'match-box nose', an unusually absurd one; one or two of the scouts have noses that simply won't fit nicely into a matchbox.

At the end the troop falls in again, sings God Save the King, and dismisses. Five minutes later the last scout has been herded out into the night, contentedly munching a bun.

Good Turns by the Swifts. Christmas Eve (from an account by Yeatman)
Yeatman, R. Pearman, Harrod and Barrett met in uniform on the afternoon of Christmas Eve with the intention of going round Burford doing good turns. (Townsend and Wilsden were unable to get off). They called at many cottages, but at first trade was very slack. Mrs Allsworth however they found busy at her housework, and only too glad to send the scouts to do her shopping for her. At Mrs Parson's, where they went next, they cleared the table, washed up, chopping the wood, fetched the coal, and did the shopping; lucky Mrs Parsons! One old lady remarked 'My word, I shall never be able to thank you scouts, you be proper gentlemen!' They finished up by doing errands for Miss Emeris and Miss Read. Well done Swifts; that's the spirit!

Tracking, Signet Wood Jan 6th (by Bayliss)
We met at the club room at 2.15pm. We suggested going track-ing and Bayliss and Pether were chosen as hares. After a quarter of an hour had elapsed we started to track them; (the blighters had forgotten to lay any trail for about the first half mile G.H.) We came across various signs till we found them preparing a camp fire about three miles away, so we joined in. This was a good camp fire on a stretch of grass by the side of a stream. It was a beautiful fine evening, but cold; we rigged up a shelter out of an old sheep hurdle and some coats, and sat round the blaze in the twilight. Hunt and Bayliss were noteworthy chaps

for fetching water from about half a mile away. After making our own tea, we enjoyed a hearty meal which we brought with us; we played some games, using Hunt's blank gun to start us off. Just after 5 o'clock we started back for home; on the way we sang songs and solos. Harrod broke Barrett's cup, which caused a disturbance. We marched into Burford, and half way down the hill the SM dismissed us.

Scout camp

We had many adventures which are described in great detail in the Log Book ie scout camps, expeditions, tracking, general troop work and rallies. We had visits from the District Commissioner, and took part in church and Armistice Day parades. We played against other Scout troops in football and boxing matches, swimming and running competitions. We put on evenings of entertainment and concerts in Burford, Holwell, Aston, Ducklington and Swinbrook for various good causes.

Being a scout was a wonderful experience. We grew in confidence and gained many skills. The last entry in the Log Book shows how much we were affected by the departure of our Scoutmaster.

Arriving home

June 17th Farewell Meeting. D. Cook

On October 11th Mr Heywood started a troop of Scouts in Burford. For nearly three years he worked with, and helped them, on June 17th 1932 he left them and soon afterwards went to China to carry on his meteorological work there. Such may be the report of an outsider, yet words cannot express what Mr Heywood did for us, it is sheer uselessness to try to explain how the Scoutmaster worked for the Troop, he only left one thing for us to do, that was carry on and keep up the standard. We will do our utmost yet one thing will be lacking, we shall not be able to run up and consult Mr Heywood in our difficulties. Yet though we may bemoan our loss let us smile, whistle, and carry on the good work as the Scout-master wishes. Though this is the most vital point in the history of the 1st Burford troop let us not give it up as a bad job. We have been shown how to carry on then let us use the gift given to us by that great benefactor, whose name we deem worthy to go down in history as a great man, Graham Heywood. Good luck, happiness and all that is best in life to our Scoutmaster at Hong-Kong.

June 18th surely was a fitting finish to the great work of Mr Heywood for the Owls to get 299 out of 300 marks in the County Flag competition on June 18th and 19th. It was a weekend of the usual competition type, one word of advice to the next Burford patrol entering this competition. Know your Tenderfoot and Second Class tests thoroughly, show a Scout Spirit and you will bring that flag back to Burford.

It was only natural that great difficulty was experienced in finding another Scoutmaster, time rolls away before one is aware and although the Troop has been struggling on, not until now (November 1933) do we feel settled down. Now we welcome Mr Drewe as Scoutmaster and although there is a difficult task before him, we feel sure he will pull us through. Many old scouts and a nice handful of recruits turned up at the resumed meetings, let us forge ahead so that when Mr Heywood rolls back to old England in 1935 he will find a first class troop waiting to welcome him home.

Life changed for me. I left school and started working for Garnes Brewery in Burford, but I didn't like it, left and went back to school.

A year or so later I got the job as window dresser at Elliston & Cavell in Oxford, and left home to lodge with an aunt in Oxford.

Chapter three

November 10 1938 – December 12 1939

1938 was a critical year for me and set the pattern of events to follow, and my contribution to the war effort.

In September 1938 I was lodging with an aunt in Oxford, together with another lad, Frank Wilcox. We both worked for a large department store in Oxford, Elliston and Cavell. I worked in the display department and Frank worked in the carpet department. The jobs were not very exciting but at least we were working, and lucky to be, because there was mass unemployment at that time.

In November 1938 rumblings of war were in the far distance, but because we wanted some excitement we decided to join the Royal Air Force Volunteer Reserves. To actually be taught to fly, and be paid for it as well, was almost unbelievable. Our shop wages were about thirty shillings a week and the extra cash would certainly make a difference.

We filled in the necessary forms and went to Kidlington Airport for the medical examinations. This took up an entire day and we both failed with ear problems. We were naturally disappointed and determined to try again. The problem had been that our ears had refused to 'pop' but with a little help from our doctor we passed a second medical a month later. We were sworn in and received the King's Shilling.

No time was wasted and very soon we were taken for our first flight. In a state of great apprehension and excitement we were taken out to an aircraft, a Miles Magister – a twin seat open cockpit. We climbed in and the little aircraft rumbled over the rough grass field, as it was then, and I remember vividly looking back and down, seeing the airport 'fall away' and the sensation of being airborne for the first time. The pilot on that trip was a Flight Lieutenant Mills and the flight lasted fifteen minutes; this was the start of our flying instruction.

This first flight covered Nos. 1 Air Experience and 2 The Effect of Controls. Later that same day we had a second trip and further instruction covering Nos. 3 Taxiing and Handling the Engine, and 4 Straight and Level Flying. This concluded my first day with the RAF Volunteer Reserves. They certainly did not waste time in training us, and on the second day we were automatically made Sergeants, and my number was 742479. All pre-war Volunteer Reserves numbers began with 742.

The next few months were hectic. We spent all our spare time flying and attending lectures at Harburton House in Headington, Oxford. The lectures were taken in the evenings, and consisted of two hourly lectures, twice a week. We cycled there, had one lecture, then a glass of beer, and then the second lecture. For this we were paid two shillings per hour plus our travelling expenses, so we put in for bus fares, even though we cycled there.

The lectures comprised Elementary Engines, Rigging, Theory of Flight, Airmanship, Navigation, Parachuting, Armaments, Signals and Drill and at the end of the course our civilian instructors made sure we all passed. Meanwhile, Frank moved to a job in London, and continued with his training there.

We were all keen to do our first solo and after ten hours of dual, we achieved it. On the day of the solo we had fifteen minutes of dual circuits and landings, and then the instructor got out and gave me last minute instructions. I taxied to the far side of the aerodrome, opened the throttle fully, keeping straight with the rudder, feeling the aircraft bumping over the rough grass. As I gained speed the tail came up and I eased back on the control column and slowly left the ground. I climbed to five hundred feet and turned left, climbed on to a thousand feet, and turned left again. On the down wind leg I passed the aerodrome.and turned left again, reduced height down to five hundred feet and finally turned into the wind and landed. What a relief to be safely back on the ground!

When war was declared in September 1939, we obviously were the first to be called up. We had to report to Oxford Town Centre for further instructions. Due to much confusion we were sent on leave on full pay, plus living out allowance. This amounted to the princely sum of nineteen shillings and sixpence per day, and we were told to report back in a week's time. This lasted for six weeks, and we reported to Kidlington airport every Friday to receive our pay from Pilot Officer Cheshire – who would become Group Captain Cheshire VC, and who was a Pilot Officer in the Oxford University Air Squadron.

Our group had a wonderful six weeks on our allowance. We went swimming, hired cars and generally lived it up. Then one day a telegram arrived ordering us to report to Oxford Town Centre, with kit, to catch a train to the Initial Training Wing at Bexhill. So with the news that we had to leave we went on one last bender. We went to a large hotel in George Street, Oxford and had a party. Steel, who owned a Morris Minor, took us to the Morris works to say farewell to his mates. Eight of us squashed into this little car, some hung on from outside and the police turned a blind eye. Needless to say when we arrived at Bexhill we were in very good spirits!

Our billet at Bexhill was the Sackville Hotel, which had been requisitioned by the RAF. Our first few days were spent filling sand bags on the beach to build a protective wall around the hotel, and the rest of the time was spent doing PT, drill and attending lectures. While I was there I found out that Frank Wilcox was at Hastings ITW, so I had the chance to look him up. Eventually, after about eight weeks, our postings came through and our class split up as we all went our various ways.

I was posted to Montrose, together with another Burford lad, Dennis Pether, and a fellow named Sandy Pate who had lodged with my mother in Burford. His father was a doctor practising in Beaumont Street, Oxford

and Sandy had worked in Lloyds Bank in Burford. (Sandy was killed early on in the war, while on a night training exercise – he apparently became lost and ran into a balloon cable).

Bob *(left)* with John

Bob *(right)* with Bertie

Chapter four

Montrose Flight Training School
December 1939 – May 10 1940

Montrose is situated on the east coast of Scotland between Aberdeen and Dundee, and this was a small First World War airfield. It was an Intermediate and Advanced Flying School, flying Airspeed Oxfords and Miles Masters. Here we were divided up to fly either single engine aircraft, or twin or multi-engine aircraft. I was selected for Oxfords. It was assumed by us that singles would be fighter pilots and twins, bomber pilots. We had not heard of any other Commands at the time.

We slept in large huts housing thirty men, and an old time Flight Sergeant was put in charge of us, and he was allocated a cubicle at the end of the hut. It was a terribly cold winter so we tried to keep the coke stove burning all night, so consequently we had to draw lots to see who would have to get out of bed in the middle of the night to keep the fire made up. If this was not done, our boots, wet with snow, would be frozen to the floor by morning.

Flying started on December 12, with dual in the Oxford, going through the usual exercises before going solo. This was followed by more dual receiving more advanced instruction in slow flying, operation flying, bad weather flying, climbing turns, forced landings, instrument flying, take-off and landings across wind, navigation, cross country and so on. Two of us trainee pilots would fly together and take it in turns to practice these exercises. Circuits and landings were not controlled by a Flying Control, therefore, Oxfords, Masters and the odd Spitfire from 603 Squadron (also based at Montrose) were landing wherever they could find a clear space on the airfield. Consequently there were a lot of near misses and a fair few accidents with aircraft landing and taking off at the same time. On reflection, seeing how flying is controlled today, to say that it was dangerous is an understatement.

An Oxford after a Spitfire has flown
through it!

Remains of a Spitfire

15

Adverse weather conditions affected the flying, especially where the Oxfords were concerned. If a white frost had covered the wings the aircraft was unable to leave the ground because the layer of frost actually altered the shape of the wings, and thereby upset the lift, so this always had to be checked before take-off.

On one occasion, within a space of four minutes, four aircraft suffered damage as they attempted to take-off. One aircraft managed to leave the ground but could not gain any height and hit a brick wall, killing Tommy Watkins, the pilot. A second aircraft just cleared the sand dunes and flew into a railway signal box wrecking both box and aircraft and injuring the pilot, Scacey. (He recovered from his injuries and was posted on. We did not see him again because he was later killed in a Hudson on Coastal Command.)

Our next important training exercise was night flying; we were required to go solo at night to get our wings.

The flare path was set out into wind across the aerodrome in the shape of a T. A taxiing post, illuminated in the shape of a Christmas tree, was near the start of the take-off position and the aircraft would be required to wait at the post until it received the green light from the Aerodrome Control Pilot on the flare path. If we had to wait at the post for any considerable time, we had to recheck the wings for white frost, and always carried a torch for this purpose.

Night flying presented other problems mainly due to the fact that this small airfield was built in the First World War for slower aircraft, and an approach over the hangar roof was pretty daunting during a first solo. After some dual and some final instruction i.e. making sure that you fly over the red light on the hangar at not less than 100 feet, I completed my first solo at night and was awarded the Flying Badge (Wings). There was no Passing Out parade and no fuss – I just got the badge from the stores and sewed it on to my jacket.

We all spent a lot of time in the hut studying for further examinations; we also did a fair amount of brass polishing, and so a little light entertainment was always welcome. Scacey dressed only in his issue underwear would ballet dance for us – he was a natural entertainer and great fun. One night, after a few drinks, a chap came in late and peed (on purpose) into Scace's flying helmet hanging on the door near his bed, and we could all hear the drip, drip, drip. Scace, as we called him, was not too happy about it although he took it in good part.

For lectures, we were divided into groups of twenty or thereabouts, with one of our trainee pilots in charge. We had to march everywhere and we were worked very hard, especially on the theory aspect. We had one hour of signals each morning, learning morse code and receiving up to twelve words a minute. We dealt with navigation in an extremely thorough way, learning definitions, forty three of them, by heart. We learnt about deviation and variation, triangle of velocities, the compass and how to swing it. We learnt about magnetic courses, compass course, magnetic dip, isobars, magnetic field, dead reckoning, plotting and so on.

We took pages of notes on the subject of rigging, most of which was useless as it mainly concerned wooden aircraft with cross wires etc. the old string bag types. The off centre principle for working the ailerons, where the one going down goes half as far as the one going up, was the only interesting bit of information on rigging. Engines – more definitions, theory of magnetos, four stroke cycle, compression ratio, flame rate, valve overlap, stress of crankshafts, journals, webbs, angles learned only for exams and forgotten immediately.

We learned about the Theory of Flight; why and how an aircraft flies, where the lift comes from, pressures and forces acting on the aircraft. Administration – hygiene and equivalent ranks, acquaintance with regulations, official secrets, responsibilities of officers, treatment of subordinates, trade groups. Armament – theory of flight, types of guns, parts of guns, gas operated guns, Browning gun – stripping a Browning gun blindfold, learning the name of every part and clearing blockages and so on. Bombing – bomb sights, time fall of bomb, trail angle, theory of bombing, all of which kept us very busy and which involved a lot of evening work if we were to pass all these exams.

Some evenings were spent either in the Mess or in a café in Montrose. One evening, after a few drinks in the Mess, the atmosphere was such that it turned into a wild party. Back in the hut a rough house started. Our mattresses were made up of three sections and these were used to make barricades at each end of the hut, and things started flying. Anything that was moveable was thrown and it was total chaos. At one time we could not see the other end of the hut. Vim was being thrown and it created a thick fog. All the bulbs and lampshades were smashed and the whole place was demolished. The Flight Sergeant in charge was furious and informed us that he would bring the Station Warrant Officer round in the morning to see the mess, and we would all be on a Charge.

Bob and Fred

We had an airman called Fred in charge of the general cleaning of our huts and for a small fee he would make our beds at night, fold our blankets in the morning and polish our bed space. We sent him down to Montrose first thing the next morning for new bulbs and shades, and he also helped us clean up the mess. When the Flight Sergeant brought round the SWO all was clean and shipshape and so no charge was brought. I think we were the only hut on the camp that could boast pink lampshades.

So what with working and playing hard, our six months at Montrose passed very quickly. We had all been keen to learn and most of us managed to pass our examinations. After being issued with webbing equipment we all waited anxiously for our next posting. I was posted to Upper Heyford near Oxford, which took me nearer home, together with Jock Nichol and Frank Ormonroyd.

Chapter five

Upper Heyford
May 11 1940 – August 5 1940

We arrived at Upper Heyford on 11 May 1940; this was our Operational Training Unit, where we were to pass out as Operational Pilots.

On arrival we went to the Sergeant's Mess to check in and find our sleeping quarters. I was placed in married quarters – these were houses originally used for RAF families but were now solely used as sleeping quarters with beds in every room. The mess itself was very small, tidy and occupied by Sergeants and Flight Sergeants, who made us feel that we were upsetting their comfortable existence. To be suddenly invaded by newly promoted Sergeants, young and noisy, was more than they could stand. It had probably taken these old regulars about eighteen years to get their Sergeant stripes, no wonder we were unpopular having received them on the second day. We ate meals only twice with them, and from then on were made to eat in the Airmen's Mess. This was the start of a great deal of ill feeling between the ground staff and aircrew, and this attitude persisted for years during the War and mainly in the old permanent stations. The atmosphere improved slowly when they saw the risks being taken, especially in the active part of the war when many of our men were killed or went missing.

Flight Sergeant Pearman

Our flying at Heyford started on 24 May 1940 (exactly forty-seven years ago, as I write this) in Navigation flight. We were given dual in the Avro Anson which was used for navigational exercises, instrument flying and one engine circuit landings and D.R plottings. We were not long in this flight, but completed twelve flights in six days and then went into Conversion flight. The aircraft we were converted to, and eventually to fly on operations, was the Handley Page Hampden Mk1. It was an all metal, midwing monoplane, powered by two Pegasus XVIII engines. It was designed and equipped for the duties of a medium bomber with a crew of four. This comprised the pilot, front gunner (who was also navigator and bomb aimer) upper rear gunner (who was also the wireless operator) and a lower rear gunner. The navigator was usually a pilot who, to gain experience, flew about six trips as a navigator before being made captain of his own aircraft.

The single fighter style cockpit of the Hampden precluded any dual, and tuition consisted of peering over the instructor's shoulder from start up to landing, noting every action. Then the instructor would get out and the pupil would take over the driving seat. We were given a board, which was strapped to the leg with instructions for before take-off, after take-off, before landing and after landing.

With the bad reputation that the Hampden had, of one engine failure at three hundred feet, you made quite sure that nothing on that board was missed.

One day sitting behind Pilot Office Simpson, I studiously memorised everything he did, and after an hour's flying it was time for me to take over. I tried not to use the throttle too much, because opening and closing the throttle would inject neat petrol into the super charger, and on take-off there would be a rich mixture going to the engine, and as soon as this mixture was exhausted and returned to normal mixture, the engine would miss and at this point usually the engine failure happened. Taxiing down wind and turning across I started checking the list on my board, HTMPFFGG – Hydraulics, Trim, Mixture, Pitch, Fuel, Flaps, Gills, Gyro. Thus, Hydraulics selected On. Trim to Take off setting. Mixture Rich. Pitch at fully fine. Fuel cocks on and fuel adequate for flight. Flaps set for take off. Gills closed after taxiing out. Gyro set to read Zero. Then making sure that all was clear for take-off, I turned into the wind, opened up the engine against the brakes and then released the brakes as the throttle was pushed fully open.

The aircraft moved forward and slowly gained speed, easing it off the ground at approximately 85 mph, raising the undercarriage, nose down to level flight until the speed of 120 mph was reached.

Return hydraulic power control to off and undercarriage selector lever to normal. Coarsing pitch to climbing revs and throttling back to $2\frac{1}{2}$lb boost, a gentle left turn and then levelling out at 1,000 feet. Pitch back to 1850 rpm and opening gills to keep cylinder head temperature normal.

A Hampden over the Channel. © Frank Wootton

A turn left and the airfield lies below and away to the left. Throttling back and holding a steady height of 1,000 feet. Reducing speed to 115 mph again going through the list on my board, supercharger flaps, hydraulic power on, undercarriage lever down, mixture normal, pitch fully forward, supercharger turning left across wind, lowering flaps, picking my landing path and reducing speed to 95 mph turn in to land, adjusting the trim to take the load off the control column. Hand on the throttle in case of undershoot, I cross the hedge, gently move the stick back until the wheels just touch the ground, closing the throttles the aircraft slowly settles with a slight bump and rolls to a stop after applying the brakes.

With a sigh of relief the first solo is completed, but more things still to do on board. Firstly raise flaps, hydraulic power control off, taxiing in and opening the gills fully to keep the air-cooled engine cool. Then pitch to coarse open engines for about a minute, then operate slow running cut out and switches off. From then on it was flying and getting used to the aircraft.

In the Advanced Training Flight we studied one engine flying, instrument flying, changing seats in the air – this was a very difficult operation, but it was just about possible by letting down the back of the pilot's seat to allow the body and legs to be withdrawn from the cockpit, and at the same time the pilot taking over would lean forward and hold the control column steady until the pilot was clear. Then the other person would slide into the pilot's seat as quickly as possible, so to gain full control of the aircraft.

Thirty-three flights in eleven days, and then on to Armament Flight. Here we practiced high and low level bombing at Otmoor Range with practice bombs, air firing at drogue targets from all gun positions. I completed fifteen flights in six days.

A crew operational flight was the final one where we flew as a full crew, day and night exercises, formation flying and low flying to prepare us for the real thing. Low flying was a part of advanced training and it was a triangular area which stretched from Heyford to Gloucester to Worcester, which of course included Burford where we were permitted to fly. Low flying is the only time one gets the impression of speed. I knew the area well and could fly at will without fear of getting lost. One favourite run was flying at the side of the A40 alongside cars at nought feet, hedge hopping and watching out for electric and telephone wires.

This I thoroughly enjoyed and really made the most of it. Low level flying without permission was regarded as a crime, but it just added to the excitement. We also used to use what we called the Iron Beam (railway line) and of course it was no problem to fly to Worcester this way. This was the last authorised low flying we did, but it was really exciting. We did eleven flights in nine days for low flying practice. This made a total of 156 hours flying in fourteen weeks.

During this time we had twenty-two crashes, fifteen pilots killed, and thirteen injured. The number killed could have been many more, as records of the crashes beyond repair did not always record injuries. The crashes were mainly due to engine failure at about 300 feet.

The young trainee pilots were marshals for funeral parades. There were many rehearsals for these and we always had to act as bearers. This was a depressing job for us to do, as it brought home the dangerous work we did.

On one occasion, a very hot day, I was one of the bearers carrying the coffin into Heyford church. I felt the perspiration running down my face and dripping from my chin; the coffin was heavy because, although we knew there was very little left of the deceased, the coffin had been filled with something weighty for the benefit of parents and family. There is not much left of a pilot after a crash followed by fire. This experience always subdued us as we always wondered who would be next. It was at this time I became aware of the huge risks involved in flying that would be even greater when we started operations. I wrote two letters, one to my mother and one to Norah, only to be opened in the event of me not returning home.

The Hampden losses were so great that they introduced the Hereford, mainly to save the Pegasus XVIII engines, which were used in a number of aircraft beside the Hampden. The Hereford was a Hampden with a Napier Dagger engine. These were fluid cooled engines and developed their take off power at 4250 rpm with cruise setting at 3500 rpm. The noise, a high pitched scream was impressive but disconcerting, after the purr of the Pegasus engines at 1800 rpm.

The Hereford was also nose heavy. Normal flying was similar to the Hampden, but it was impossible to make a three point landing and you had to be content with wheelers. These were only flown in the daytime by pupils.

At Heyford I saw a lot more of my fiancé, Norah. My old Triumph, which had been on blocks at Burford, was brought back into use and although petrol was rationed, it was possible to obtain extra. A civilian in the Mess would borrow the car for the evening and bring it back full of petrol. It was a rather good arrangement and enabled me to see more of Norah, nicknamed Bill, and all my off duty time was spent with her.

A friend named Jock Nichol was friendly with a girl called Paddy from Charlbury, and we would make up a foursome and Norah would stay at Charlbury. Our arrangement for meeting was usually the same; we would meet the girls in Oxford one hour after flying over the house in Charlbury. At the back of the house were fields sloping away and down and this enabled us to make a low approach over the house so that they would recognise us and make their way to Oxford.

Jock and I flew together as a pair, flying alternate trips as pilot/navigator so we always arrived back at the same time. My memory of Heyford is that it seemed to be always hot and sunny and the four of us spent many evenings boating on the river at Oxford, getting back to the station in the early hours of the morning. On one occasion I arrived back just in time to fetch the aircraft from dispersal to the hangar at about 6.30am. We made the most of our free time not knowing what lay ahead, or how long we would stay at Heyford.

One day the Station Commander called everyone together in the station cinema to warn us of an expected invasion at any moment; it was at the time of Dunkirk. Although we had no weapons, we were expected to defend the station to the best of our ability. All the guns on the aircraft were manned twenty-four hours a day; each Sergeant Pilot together with four airmen had to see that they were organised into taking it in turns to guard each aircraft all night. Had Hitler invaded at this time he could have walked in without a shot being fired. I was not issued with a firearm until 1943.

Looking back through my Log Book, I see that I flew with a man called Frank Ormonroyd several times at Heyford, and did not see him again until a few years ago when I spotted him on television, in a programme about British Airways Flying Control where he was working – so he had survived the war. Following that I located him and we chatted on the phone about days gone by. It was here that I met Charles Gibson, with whom I took it in turns night flying in the Anson and worked with him for the next few months.

At last the posting came through and mine was to Finningley in Yorkshire, which was a holding unit before postings to the squadron. I was sorry to leave Heyford for many reasons, and of course it meant that I would not see Norah for some time. I was also relieved to be away from the flying side of it for a while, for the loss of pilots and aircraft had been a terrible eye-opener for me. It had been a real initiation into the serious side of flying in the war.

This portrait of Bob was painted by David Rowlands, who is a well-known military artist. He was a close friend of Steve (Bob's second son) who commissioned this work for his dad.

Chapter six

Finningley
5 August 1940 – 20 August 1940
I arrived at Finningley on August 5 1940 where we were kept occupied with practice bombings and cross country trips. From there we were posted to our squadrons on August 20 1940. I was sent to 144 Squadron at Hemswell.

144 Squadron

Hemswell
20 August 1940 to 8 April 1941
On the first night I went to a concert in one of the hangars given by an ENSA party. It seemed like another world especially knowing no-one there, and with one or two crews dressed in flying gear ready for operations having a quick glance at the concert before taking off. It was at this point I knew that the serious side of the war had started for me.

Eventually I was to be crewed up with a Sergeant Walker, as his navigator. A Sergeant Wetherill was the wireless operator and top gunner, and a Sergeant Turner, bottom air gunner. It is difficult to remember the events of each trip, but our debriefing notes are still kept at the Air Ministry and I have managed to obtain copies of the actual notes relating to each trip.

De-briefing notes taken from the AM Operations Record Book.

Our first trip was to Mannheim on September 2 1940. The report reads:

> We set course from Lincoln at 300 feet an airspeed of 150mph. At 2215 hours crossed the English coast but unable to pinpoint position. From here we climbed and at 2245 hours reached 10,000 feet. The Dutch coast appeared at 2250 and was still unable to pinpoint position. It was a very dark night and map reading was impossible so we decided to set course for Base and jettison our bombs into the sea. We crossed the English coast at 0210 hours and landed at Scampton at 0330 hours. *Trip 6 hours 10 min.*

Picking out targets at night was very nearly impossible unless near a river. One could at times, make out the difference between land and water. In the early days of the war we were not allowed to do any indiscriminate bombing and if the target was not found, bombs had to be brought back or jettisoned safely into the sea.

The next trip was to a synthetic oil factory at Politz near Stetin, north east of Berlin. As this was a long trip we had to fly to Marham in Norfolk for refuelling. This was another chance to look up Frank Wilcox who was stationed there on 38 Squadron, flying Wellington bombers.

The de-briefing notes are as follows:
> At 2021 hours set course from Marham and started climbing to 10,000 feet. At 2041 we crossed the German coast where we pinpointed ourselves and found that we were on course. We arrived at the target area at 2330 hours and found the target which was well on fire. We dropped our stick of bombs just to the left of the fire which started another one, which could be seen for about thirty minutes after leaving. We obtained a fix otherwise the journey was uneventful. We landed back at Marham at 0345 hours. *Trip 7 hours 30 minutes.*

The next four trips were also straightforward. The first was to bomb the barges in the Channel ports, which were preparing for the invasion of England. Although this was a nice short trip, they were well defended and it was a case of fly in, drop the bombs and get out as quickly as possible. Being young and keen I suggested to Sergeant Walker that we went in low so that I could 'have a go' at the search lights. Being navigator I had a Browning gun, and by opening a small trap door in the floor I could push the gun through and hold firm with my two feet. Sergeant Walker had more sense and told me in fairly plain language to give him a course to steer for home.

Arriving back at Hemswell we called by radio for permission to land. The reply came back that German aircraft were in the circuit. If we could land without lights and flare path we had their permission to try. We could just make out the boundary hedge in the darkness, so the approach was made switching on the aircraft landing light just before crossing the hedge, making a perfect landing. This was a grass airfield and so we were not limited to a specific runway.

It was a nasty habit of the Germans to join our aircraft in the circuit and have a shot at us either in the circuit, or just when landing. At that time the Whitleys were in Yorkshire, Hampdens in Lincolnshire, Wellingtons in East Anglia (Norfolk, Suffolk, Cambridgeshire) so it was easy for them to intercept the return when they knew what types of aircraft were bombing. Fighters would be sent from France to patrol different counties.

The de-briefing notes for this trip and the next three are as follows:

Ostende September 7 – Barges

We were airborne at base at 2035 hours and set course from Lincoln at 2040 hours. After pinpointing ourselves in the Wash we found we were on track and crossed the coast at Aldeburgh. We arrived at the enemy coast at 2150 hours. It was just possible to pick out the coastline, so we followed it down looking for the target. There was a ground haze and we found what we thought to be the target area, but could not be quite sure. This search carried on for an hour and a half and in the end we decided to jettison our bombs in the sea and set course for base, which we did. Landing at 0130 hours.   *Trip 4 hours 50 minutes*

Calais September 10 – Barges

At 2030 hours we were airborne at base and set course from Lincoln at 2034. At the Wash we pinpointed ourselves and found that we were on course. We crossed the English coast at 2115 hours and arrived at target area at 2135 hours. We could just manage to see the docks through the searchlight glare, but could not pick out the barges. So we dropped our stick of bombs across the dock. The result of the bombs could not be seen owing to

Bombing the barges. Chris Stoddart © 44 Squadron RAF

intense searchlight glare, but the bursts were observed which were definitely in the target area. On arriving at base we were greeted by anti-aircraft fire which was meant for enemy aircraft which were somewhere in the district. Finding it impossible to get anywhere near the aerodrome we decided to land at Waddington which we did at 0035 hours. *Trip 3 hours 35 minutes*

Dunkirk September 14 – Barges

We were airborne at base at 1955 hours and set course from Lincoln at 2002 hours. At 2051 hours we crossed the English coast on our outward journey and arrived in the target area at 2130 hours. The searchlights and anti-aircraft fire was intense but we were able to recognise the target area. We made three attempts to drop our bombs but the fire was so intense that we were obliged to make a fourth run-in. This was done with the engines throttled back. The bombs were dropped in the target area but owing to the avoiding action taken by the pilot it was impossible to see the bursts. The journey home was uneventful and we landed at base at 2320 hours. *Trip 4 hours 15 minutes*

Le Havre September 18 – Barges

We were airborne at base at 1932 hours and set course from Lincoln at 1937 hours crossing the coast on outward journey was made at 2012 hours. Soon after the pilot informed me that he was feeling ill and did not feel like carrying on with the rest of the trip. It seemed a pity to bring our bombs back so we decided to drop them on Dunkirk. There were large fires on the quayside so we decided to bomb them in the hope of them spreading. The bombs were seen to burst just to the left of the fire on the dock-side. We left the target area at 2055 hours and arrived back at base at 2229 hours, the pilot reported sick on landing. *Trip 3 hours 15 minutes*

It was in October 1940 that I first had my own aircraft and crew. The navigator was a Sergeant Streeter, with two Sergeant Turners, one top rear gunner and wireless operator and the other lower rear gunner, or as we used to call it, one in the tin. This was a mine laying trip which was referred to as 'gardening' and this was considered a quiet first trip.

So with a total of 16.45 solo night flying hours to my credit, I was on my first operation. The aircraft were dispersed in fields around the airfield on hard standings. The crew were taken out in a truck for the night flying test, to check that everything was in order for the trip. We then had to bring the

Loading a mine onto a Hampden. © Michael Turner. Studio 88

aircraft to the hangar apron for loading the mine. After switching off the engines I sat in the cockpit waiting for the mine to arrive. Suddenly there was a flash and a thudding explosion behind the hangar and I realised that it was my mine. It was being towed by a tractor and loaded on a bomb trolley; the tractor driver and the armourers riding on the mine totally disappeared, and there was very little left of the tractor and trolley. Three minutes delay in exploding and I would not be here either. This was a pretty unnerving incident to happen just before my first operation.

These particular mines were magnetic and fused by a naval officer stationed with us for that purpose. More armourers were found, another mine fused and loaded, and I taxied out very slowly to dispersal with very great apprehension. We first had to attend a briefing, which consisted of the met man giving details of the weather, wind speed, direction etc., the signals officer then gave codes and call signs for the radio operator and any information on what to expect in the way of search lights etc., the colours of the day for the cartridges. We were told that we had to drop the mine from 300 feet to prevent it from breaking up on impact, at a point in Kiel Bay where shipping had to round. The navigator was given a target map and all was set.

The trip was very quiet. Flying over Denmark we could see the odd search light to the south, sweeping the sky for intruders. On approaching the target area we started losing height dropping down to 300 feet. The point where we were to plant the mine was near. Bomb doors opened and the navigator called over the intercom – I repeated 'bomb door open, master switch on and bomb selected'. The navigator gave me the final directives before the drop, left … left … steady … right … steady … then a long pause … I was expecting the call 'bombs gone' to come through the intercom. But instead the navigator announced that we had a hang up. Again we tried a second run, making sure the selector switches were all correct, and second time, a hang up. We tried a shallow dive on the third attempt, but still the mine stayed firmly fixed to the aircraft. We had no alternative but to bring it back, and hope that it stayed firmly attached to the aircraft on landing.

We had a steady but quiet flight home. On the final approach at Hemswell, the flare path nicely lined up, the engine note rose as the pitch went to fully fine – the flare path suddenly blacked out. I instantly thought that the Luftwaffe were on the circuit. Peering into the darkness it suddenly became extremely alarming – I could just identify the differing shades of darkness of the sky and land and could just make out the stark silhouette of trees against the sky. Expecting to hit the ground at any moment I opened the throttle fully to gain height for another attempt. The flare path suddenly reappeared – it had not gone out – I had failed to increase my approach speed to counter the extra load and the higher rate of sink. A barrier of trees lay between the aircraft and the airfield and I just managed to clear these.

On the next attempt I brought the aircraft in at a much higher speed and touched down just before the last flare. Fierce braking to reduce speed, a final swerve to avoid the boundary wall, which I knew was very near – hoping and praying that the rough treatment would not upset the mine. I taxied to dispersal. It had not been an auspicious start, with all the bad luck we had had, but we had got away with it.

Kiel October 2 1940 – Mine Laying (First Trip as Pilot)

Set course from base at 1927 hours. Reached target without difficulty at 2305 hours. We were unable to release our mine owing to wiring fault. We spent twenty minutes trying to release it. At 2324 hours set course for base where we landed at 0240 hours still carrying the mine.

A large number of crashes and losses in Bomber Command were due to inexperience, not knowing how to cope in emergencies, getting lost and running short of fuel. Coping with the bad winter weather, and the fact that they were all night trips also didn't help. So my first trip certainly taught me a lot, the main point being that the stalling speed increases with the load carried, and I never forgot this. My solo night flying hours amounted to 23 hours and 20 minutes. Mines were extremely temperamental and quite a number exploded in flight, and we had no idea what effect electrical storms would have on them. I remember seeing a mine exploding at Scampton bomb dump about seven miles away and what a spectacular sight that was. It was the only mine laying trip I did and I was not sorry.

The next trip to Essen was cut short because of icing up.

Essen October 9 1940

We set course at 1843 hours. After severe icing we reached target area. At 2050 hours owing to low cloud we were unable to find

the target, but at 2105 hours we bombed an aerodrome and set
course for base.   *Trip 4 hours 35 minutes*

The next two trips were uneventful, one to Merseburg and one to Hanover.

Merseburg October 16 1940

Set course at 1845 hours but after crossing the enemy coast flew
over 10/10 cloud to within 40 miles of target area. Under these
circumstances we did not find the target but bombed a large
factory. At 2155 hours set course for base. The weather was very
bad and we landed at 0200 hours at Honington.

Time 8 hours 20 minutes

Hanover October 25 1940

Set course at 0013 hours but were unable to identify target,
though we searched the area above 8/10 cloud from 0400 hours
until 0432 hours, so we bombed an aerodrome and set course for
base which we reached at 0700 hours.   *Time 6 hours*

Following these were two trips to Berlin. Berlin was fairly easy to find
because the Germans would put up a heavy barrage, and to bomb I had
to fly through the barrage. It was said that the barrage they put up,
together with all the search lights, was around six or seven miles north of
Berlin so we may not have done the damage we thought.

Berlin October 26 1940

Set course 2324 hours and reached Berlin at 0325 hours. We
could not find the target owing to low cloud. At 0355 we set
course for base and obeyed instructions and regretfully jettisoned our bombs on the return journey. We landed at 0750
hours.   *Trip 8 hours 35 minutes*

The last Berlin trip on October 29 1940 was where I first experienced static
electricity. We were in a thick haze when the static started. Two blue rings
suddenly appeared around the tip of the propeller ('St Elmo's Fire') and
from all the metal parts of the windscreen minute hair like flashes
danced. Not having seen this before we was at a loss to know what to do
about it. We were flying at 5000 feet which was quite low, and it was there
that we found ourselves over Hamburg. We could recognise this by the
flak barrage and search lights. I told the navigator to let the bombs go and
we got out as fast as possible. It was not safest place to be at that height.
The static lasted about two hours and ceased as we crossed the North Sea
on the way home.

Berlin October 29 1940

Set course at 2040 hours. Pinpointed at 2327 hours and altered course for target. We dropped our razzles and soon after encountered cumulus nimbus cloud. We descended from 15,000 feet to 13,000 feet in an attempt to get through. Experiencing severe ice, snow and static electricity we altered course at 0027 hours for Hamburg where at 0045 we successfully attacked the docks. The flak was intense and accurate but at 0350 we landed at base undamaged.   *Trip 7 hours 30 minutes*

Chapter seven

Norah and I fixed our wedding date for November 11 1940 to be held in Worcester. John, my brother, could not get time off to attend and the only guests would be Norah's mother, father and sister, my mother and the best man and his wife. However, on November 8 I was detailed for Munich operations. It was going to be a long trip and the weather report was not good. Being a Sergeant Pilot I was to be the only one from the station to go. The target was minimal; we had an extra wing tank fitted to enable us to reach our target.

The trip out was quiet, flying at about 10,000 feet. Arriving at the target area I spotted the Alps towering above us. We had overshot the target and as we were above 10/10 cloud, we dropped our bombs into some search lights and set course for home. Soon after leaving the target, trouble developed. The port engine suddenly increased its speed and a shower of sparks streamed from the exhaust. Then as suddenly as it had happened, it returned to normal. It was at this point that I told my crew of my intentions. If the engine failed we would continue as far as possible on one engine and then bale out, heading for the shortest sea crossing over the Channel.

We managed to make it back to base by following the east coast out at sea, until we spotted the Cromer lighthouse and set course from there. Arriving at base, one of the engines spluttered and stopped. It was difficult to maintain height on a single engine and the side slip of the Hampdens was well known. It was impossible not to overshoot in the event of a missed approach on landing. It was better to save the crew and abandon the Hampden. So after calling up the crew and giving the order 'prepare to abandon aircraft', I told each one to jump, and after ensuring that they had all gone, I disconnected my oxygen tube, pulled out the plug of my intercom from under my straps, slid back the canopy and made sure that I was not connected by anything to the aircraft. I then dived towards the port engine – I felt my shoulder hit the wing and then fall off the trailing edge one … two … three … pull the cord.

Floating down under the canopy I looked down, but it was dark and difficult to assess how long it would be before I hit the ground. It came sooner than expected and I found myself in a heap on the ground. Recovering the parachute and rolling it into a small bundle I started to walk, soon realising that I had damaged a knee. I went through a gate and followed the line of a hedge, until suddenly I spotted a farmhouse. It was strange that there were no boundaries to its garden and I walked straight from the field to the front door. It was Harpswell Grange. I asked to use the telephone to ring back to base whose concern was for the safety of the crew only – not the aircraft.

Munich November 8 1940

At 1820 hours we were airborne and found the target without much difficulty. We bombed and set course for base. Ten minutes after leaving the target the starboard engine cut out, so we returned via Calais, Dover, Orfordness for the sake of a short sea crossing. We reached base at 0250 hours but at 0300 both engines cut right out so we abandoned aircraft and landed safely. The aircraft was completely written off.   *Trip 9 hours 50 minutes*

After debriefing I reported sick and was due to go on leave as from that moment. But the MO was dubious about letting me go on leave as I might not come back, but when I told them I was getting married and promised to return, they relented.

I changed my clothes and hitchhiked to Worcester. This was in the early hours of the morning and there was very little traffic on the road. I was eventually given a lift by a man, who later turned out to be a reporter, and conversation turned to the raid of the previous night. I told him that I thought we had been bombing railway yards, but he told me that Hitler had been the target and apparently the raid was laid on to upset his celebrations and sent him scurrying to his shelter.

Coventry had their blitz on November 14, and it was reputed to be a reprisal ordered by Hitler for this minor raid I had made on Munich that night – the birthplace of Nazism. I looked up the Bomber Command Diaries for the activities of Bomber Command on November 9 the night of the raid and nothing was mentioned, so I wondered if I had been the only aircraft sent from England on the raid that night.

Two days later Norah and I were married and we spent one night in the Flying Horse in Nottingham. I had to return to the base by midday. Leave always ended at midday. The honeymoon consisted of the one night and

then an early train from Nottingham to Hemswell. This was one of the worst partings during the war and one I shall never forget – making the most of every second – the train pulling out of the station, Norah waving and getting smaller and smaller, wondering if we would see each other again – we both felt very lonely. The aircrew losses on the station were heavy and faces seen regularly in the Mess would suddenly not be there any more, realisation slowly dawning on you that they had gone for good.

Before an operation we were very apprehensive and at times frightened not knowing what lay ahead, but once in the air and the team working together, the feelings disappeared because we were concentrating on the job in hand. I had great faith in my crew, Streeter as navigator, Turner as wireless operator who knew his job inside out and got us home with just the radio on many occasions. Navigation was quite tricky if the wind speed and direction given at the briefing were not accurate; the navigation was haywire unless you could pinpoint a landmark, which in the dark was not easy.

We did two more trips to Dusseldorf; on one of these we were to take razzles. Razzles were phosphorous discs about four inches in diameter and they were kept in tins of water. If they dried out they would start burning. These were dropped at various intervals across Germany in the hope of setting fire to crops and in fact anything that burned. The bottom rear gunner had a metal shute fitted for dropping these razzles and occasionally one would blow back into the tail boom. If it was impossible to reach, a bucket of water and a stirrup pump had to be used to keep the razzle wet for the duration of the trip.

Dusseldorf December 5 1940

Set course for target and reached Antwerp at 0507 hours. We altered course for Dusseldorf but were forced down to low altitude by ice and snow. At 0532 we altered course for base. Our bombs were jettisoned safely into the sea. We landed at 0830 hours. *Trip 5 hours 15 minutes*

Dusseldorf December 7 1940

Set course for target and climbed to 4000 feet. Ice forced us down and we crossed the North Sea at 700 feet to Zeebrugge.

We found we could not carry on and attacked ships moored by the mole at Zeebrugge. Our bombs would not release. We decided not to risk that target again since it was a last resort, and set course for Ostende. We made two runs on the harbour but our bombs would not come off. On the second run we were forced down to sea level. We flew home at 500 feet and landed at 2230 hours.

At this time various towns in the country were being blitzed and it was decided to try the Hampdens as nightfighters. The navigator had a gun, the pilot had a fixed gun; they cut two holes in the side of the fuselage for a beam gunner, and the two rear gunners had twin guns each.

We were given height and course to fly in a V formation. One side of the V would fly at 1000 feet and the other at 500 feet, so that there would be no collisions. We were to circle Oxford and they would inform us by radio which town was being attacked.

One particular night on December 11 1940 it was Birmingham. We flew back and started patrolling at our allotted height – all the crew peering into the darkness looking for German bombers. All that we saw was Birmingham taking a battering from the Luftwaffe. My heater packed up and consequently my microphone froze up. I could not communicate with the crew and so we headed back to base – an unsuccessful trip and very cold.

Fighter Patrol over Birmingham December 11 1940
> We set course for Birmingham and patrolled our area from 2004 hours to 2158 hours. We saw two enemy aircraft but they were not at our height and were far too fast for us to attack. The intercommunication and heating failed, so we left the area and landed at 2250 hours. *Trip 3 hours 45 minutes*

Today, November 20 1987, I received a phone call from a chap who is researching 144 Squadron. He said that he was acquainted with a Mr Wiggall who flew with me in the early days. On checking my Log Book I see that he was the fifth member of my crew, the beam gunner on this trip. He only flew with me once and about a month later was shot down and was a prisoner of war for the rest of the War.

December 19 was our next trip and the target was Cologne. Weather conditions were not very good and we returned after two and three quarter hours owing to icy conditions.

Cologne December 19 1940
After take-off the weather conditions were unfavourable, drizzle, cloud base 1000 feet with 3/10 cloud at 300 feet and very dark. We set course direct for the target and climbed to 4000 feet after leaving the coast. Severe icing was experienced which gradually increased. At 0504 hours, when approximately in position, we decided to turn for base. We landed at base at 0615 hours.

Trip 2 hours 45 minutes

A trip on December 21 to Leipzig followed and there were no more trips before Christmas.

Leipzig December 21 1940
Airborne at 0030 hours and immediately set course for the Dutch coast. We pinpointed ourselves north of Amsterdam and set course for the target. Flying at 12,000 feet above 10/10 cloud we arrived above the target area. The cloud did not break however, and was too low to enable us to go below with safety so dropped our bombs in the target area. Setting course for base at 0430 hours. We arrived safely back at 0745 hours.

Trip 7 hours 15 minutes

At this time I was friendly with a chap called Arther Osborne, Ossie, and we fixed up to rent a bungalow together so that we could have our wives with us, and live away from the station. The day after Joan and Norah arrived, Ossie and I were fixed up for operations that night, the target being Bordeaux. This was to be a long trip and we were loaded with bombs at base and were to refuel at St Eval in Cornwall.

On arrival at St Eval I checked the wind direction and saw that it was blowing up a short runway. The runway was uneven, humpbacked and having a bomb load on board and from previous experience I brought the aircraft in at a faster speed than normal, touched down at the highest point and started speeding down the slight slope downhill. The far hedge loomed up far too quickly and there was no way that I could stop with the load on board. I braked hard and kicked on the right hand rudder, which caused the aircraft to swing violently to the right. This ripped off the undercarriage and we ploughed on the underbelly of the aircraft, over a gun post, through a hedge and finished up on the road.

Knowing how these aircraft would ignite at the least knock we all disembarked at high speed. We could see the bombs poking out from under the aircraft as the bomb doors had been ripped off, so we ran until we had got a good distance away. As we were running someone was running equally as fast towards us – he turned out to be a fellow member of the Oxford V.R.'s who had joined at the same time and been in the same class, a Sergeant Smith. He shouted 'Were you in that?' I replied 'Yes, but we'll discuss this elsewhere'! He was stationed at St. Eval in Coastal Command.

After every crash we had to report sick, and although no crew members were hurt we spent the night in sick quarters. Needless to say we did not do the trip to Bordeaux, but Ossie went. In the morning I went to find Ossie to check that he was OK. We had now got our wives installed and so we were keen to know that he had arrived back safely. But there was no sign of him. At hourly intervals I went to the ops room to check for news on him but nothing came. I had visions of returning to Lincoln to break the news to his wife that he was missing. Eventually at about 1.30 pm news came through that he had landed in a field near Birmingham, short of fuel and radio not working. All open fields had stakes dug in them to prevent aircraft from landing, but Ossie had managed to land. After we got back to base he told me that he had been home to Birmingham for breakfast.

We all settled into a bungalow at Walesby near Market Rasen, about twelve miles from camp. I left my old Triumph for our wives to use and Ossie had an SS Jag and also a sporty red Triumph Dolomite, which we used to go back and forth to the station. When we were on operations we would drive out to dispersal to pick up our aircraft and when we arrived back, Ossie 's car would be filled up with aviation petrol (green). This was quite risky and when the snow was on the ground there would be a telltale green patch on the ground where his carburettor had leaked. Fortunately he was never caught.

When we were on operations we used to let our wives know when we would be back by radio. We would fly over the bungalow at a very low height; they would run in and tune into the radio short-wave 47m and we would call them up on the R. T. from the aircraft so that it would not be recognised as a private chat. I used to call 'This is R. Robert calling Winfrith (the name of the house) back at such a time' depending on how long the trip was and the time of take-off.

In January we did two trips – one to Brest on January 4 and one to Gelsenkirchen on January 9. There was very little flying due to adverse weather conditions and we had one week off in six.

To fool the Germans, lots of dummy flare paths were laid out in different parts of the country. They resembled the correct path but were laid out over fields, ditches, walls in fact anywhere where the landing would be impossible. I came across one on one occasion when we were lost. After signalling for permission to land I was given a red lamp, permission was not forthcoming. Then the navigator spotted balloons all round us and above. I fired off the colours for the night with the pistol and immediately the search lights came on and shone straight up lighting up the balloons. We were in the middle of balloon barrage. At least we knew where we were and managed to climb out without any mishap and set course for base not very far away.

Brest January 4 1941

We took off from base at 1738 hours under good weather conditions and proceeded to Brest via Upper Heyford and Chesil Beach. Flying at 2000 feet below 7/10 cloud. At 2500 feet we crossed the English coast at 1833 hours. Shortly after this the cloud became 10/10 and we climbed above it to 10,000 feet descending in the target area to 8000 feet. We carried out a reconnaissance of the target area for fifteen minutes in an attempt to find a break in the cloud. At 1958 we released our bombs. At the time of release we were subjected to moderately intense heavy and light flak through the cloud layer with fair accuracy. The return journey was uneventful and we landed at base at 2255 hours. *Trip 5 hours 25 minutes*

Gelsenkirchen January 9 1941

Arriving in the target area we picked up the autobahn and the railway line north west of the target. We made our run from north west to south east but broke off the attack owing to intense opposition. We circled and commenced a second run on a reciprocal course having definitely identified the target. The flak was so intense that the aircraft was being rocked very badly by shells bursting very close and at the time of release was being thrown about very violently. As a result our bombs burst on the railway immediately to the left of the target. There was a tremendous explosion from our 1000lb and 2 x 500lb bombs and a considerable amount of debris was flying into the air. The return journey was uneventful and we landed safely at base at 0055 hours. We had one very good fix which we received in record time but this was not needed owing to good navigation in moonlight conditions. *Trip 5 hours 15 minutes*

Chapter eight

In February we flew to Brest and Mannheim. Brest was an eventful trip. On the return the radio nearly packed up and we had not had sight of the ground since we left base, so we were flying above cloud on DR. (dead reckoning). Bombs were released on search lights but we could not tell where they hit. On the way back with the last spot of power on the radio I asked for an SOS fix as the battery was running out in the radio; it came back as a third class fix which really was not much use. We plodded on using the dead reckoning until, according to our navigator, we should be over our aerodrome. Dead Reckoning means that if you fly in a certain direction at so many miles per hour for so long, you should be at point x. You then add on to that position the wind speed and direction for that time, and you should be where you expect to be. If the wind speed and direction are not correct (as supplied by the Met Office) then in six hours flying we could be a long way from where we should be.

Anyway the navigator worked out our position, which put us over our base on DR. It was getting light and above 10/10 strato cumulus. I did not want to break cloud without knowing our exact position, so I decided to fly due east 090° for one hour which should put us over the North Sea. This we did and there was nothing left for us to do but take a chance and come down; we could then get a pinpoint on the coast and set a course for home from there. We reduced height and finally broke cloud at 1000 feet over the Pennines fortunately in a valley. From there it was a case of map reading back to Hemswell. We were very lucky to break cloud where we did, because it could have quite easily been the end for us all.

Brest February 3 1941

We took off from base in a slight snowstorm at 0310 hours. Cloud base 1000 feet weather over England 10/10 cloud with base at 1000 feet. We climbed through the cloud at Bicester and proceeded by DR to the target. Weather over the English Channel 10/10 strato cumulus top 6000/7000 feet. Base not known. As we approached the French coast the clouds broke slightly and considerable flak activity was observed all along the coast. Skirting the coast we approached the target from the West.

Brest was identified by DR and by the intense flak activity. Actually over the larger area there was 9/10 cloud strato cumulus with top 6000/7000 to base estimated to be 1000/2000 feet. Owing to the cloud and darkness we did not identify the particular objective. Guided by flak fire we made our run from south to north and at 0534 hours we dropped 4 x 500lb Semi Armour Piercing (SAP) and 2 x 250lb S.A.P. from 10,000 feet. We did not observe the bursts. No fires were observed in the vicinity of the target area. We set course for base at 0540 hours and experienced weather conditions similar to those existing on the outward journey. We landed safely at base at 0905 hours.

Trip 6 hours 5 minutes

The next trip was Mannheim. It was a case of dropping the bombs in the middle of the flak and search lights. I used to drop my seat as low as possible and glue my eyes on the instruments in case I was caught in a search light cone, and get in and out of the target area as quickly as possible. On the return the weather was not good and a spot of engine trouble began. I crossed the North Sea at the shortest crossing making for the Norfolk coast, and after crossing the coastline the engine ceased to function, so we prepared to abandon aircraft. Calling out the crew one by one to jump, I got out at about 1000 feet. The aircraft burst into flames as it hit the ground and it felt as if I was floating helplessly down into the flames. I ended up in a chicken run in total darkness and desperately tried to find my way out. I made a fair racket and the owner came out with a twelve bore, and asked if I was British, then let me out. He then made me some breakfast. The rest of the crew were scattered over a wide distance, and after the phoning the nearest RAF station, Horsham St. Faith, we were packed into a truck and returned to Hemswell by late afternoon.

I looked at my aircraft on the following day and found it spread over a hundred yards between two Nissen huts where the army were sleeping, in the grounds of Tavenham Hall, Norfolk. It must have given them some nasty moments in the middle of the night!

Mannheim February 8 1941

From our take-off at base until our return to the English coast we never saw a sign of the ground, nor did we see any flak there being 10/10 cloud the whole way, tops at 6000 feet. We did not drop our bombs on ETA(estimated time of arrival) because we hoped to see something recognisable on the way home, but we did not succeed in this, and finally had to jettison over Germany, exact position unknown. We could not even see the flash of the bursts through the cloud. When over Great Witchingham, near Norwich, the starboard engine petered out and then came in again. This repeated several times then finally the engine cut out. The de-icing switch was pressed, but without effect, in any case we did not think icing conditions existed at the time, although the aircraft was in cloud. We abandoned aircraft by parachute and all landed safely. The aircraft crashed near Norwich just missing some buildings (Tavenham Hall).

Trip 5 hours and 15 minutes

While this was going on, Ossie's wife Joan and Norah were back at the bungalow waiting for us to return. We had of course let them know roughly what time to expect us. Norah told me that although they were obviously both concerned that we had not arrived back by morning, neither had mentioned it to the other, and they just kept themselves busy. Nine o'clock passed, then ten and by midday neither could stand it any longer so they phoned the base for news. Norah was told that I had baled out over Norfolk and that apparently Ossie had got lost and was guided down by Spitfires near Newmarket. We both arrived home eventually.

Before operations we had to do an N.F.T (Night Flying Test) on the aircraft to make sure that everything was serviceable on the aircraft for the night trip. A list of crews would be posted on the notice board and the time for crews to be in the briefing room. On this particular night, we assembled in the briefing room and were addressed by Bomber Harris of Bomber Command. He stood on the platform and looked around at the aircrew assembled before him and remarked 'I don't see so many of the old faces here', a fairly tactless remark to crews getting ready to fly into the unknown.

I returned from ops early one morning, and upon landing and dispersing the aircraft I was told to report to the Control Tower. This I did and was introduced to Lord Trenchard, Marshall of the Royal Air Force. After a short chat about the trip we went on to debriefing. As a young Sergeant pilot, I had never heard of Lord Trenchard, but later learned that he was one of the founders of the RAF.

Debriefing consisted of making a report on the night's events, re searchlights, position of flak guns, any enemy aerodromes we had seen and this would all be written down and read back to us. We would sign it and then go the Mess for a meal and then bed. These reports are kept in the Public Records Office at Kew, now the National Archives.

We were not worried by the German bombers very much. On one occasion they dropped a load of incendiaries near the petrol dump, but no damage was done and on another occasion they dropped an H.E. (High Explosion) bomb in the corner of the barrack square, which caused a lot of excitement. Everyone was kept well away from the area because it had not exploded. The Armourment Officer decided to blow it up, and although we kept our distance, we were still showered with dirt and rubble. No damage was done, just a hole in the square which needed to be filled in.

We did two more trips in February – one to Hanover and one to Dusseldorf.

Hanover February 11 1941

We took off from base at 1740 hours and set off in formation in daylight. We broke formation at 1842 hours just as it was getting dark and we were nearing the Dutch coast. Owing to haze and wisps of cloud we did not see the Dutch coast. This gradually became worse developing into 10/10 strato cumulus. Shortly after reaching the target the cloud cleared and the target was visible in the moonlight. We made our run from south east to north west dropping our bombs from 10,000 feet. The rear gunner could see nine fires burning in the town as we left. We encountered cloud again coming back and we did not see the English coast, tops of cloud being 7000 feet. 'Darkies', radio direction beam, proved very helpful to us as Wyton answered immediately and gave us height and cloud base. We set course for Wyton getting QDMs (a magnetic course to steer) from base, where we landed at 2307 hours.   *Trip 5 hours 45 minutes*

Dusseldorf February 25 1941

We set off from Hemswell and climbed steadily over the North Sea to 1000 feet. Turned in ETA at the Dutch coast but were unable to pinpoint our position owing to 7/10 cloud at 2000 feet. We pinpointed our position in the Rhine six miles south of Wesel and were able to pick up the river all the way to Dusseldorf, but were unable to see the town clearly owing to haze. After searching for ten minutes we were just able to locate the town by pinpointing ourselves by the river. We dropped our bombs from

11,000 feet and the bomb bursts and the incendiaries were just visible through the haze. The flak fire was not intense and seemed to be concentrated near the east side of the town. The journey back was uneventful except in the area east of Kampen where searchlights were apparently co-operating with enemy fighters. We landed at base without difficulty.

Trip 5 hours 5 minutes

In March we did three more trips – Cologne, Berlin and Dusseldorf

Cologne March 1941

A delayed start was made at 2158 hours owing to a defect on the intercom which was eventually traced to a faulty helmet. Weather conditions at base 5/10 cloud at 1000 feet. 10/10 cloud at 2000 feet raining. Setting course for Overflakee we attempted to climb through the cloud but we had not succeeded in doing so at a height of 12,000 feet. Across the North Sea we were flying blind and at 2230 hours we began to experience severe static. This was intense so we decided to abandon the operation and at 2316 hours turned for base. We jettisoned our bombs safely. On the return flight static was experienced for the whole flight back to the English coast. We landed at base at 0020 hours.

Trip 2 hours 40 minutes

Berlin March 12 1941

Taking off from base at 2140 hours we crossed the North Sea in excellent weather conditions and made landfall near Meldorf. Altering course, we proceeded to Berlin via Ratzburger Lake and as we approached Berlin we could see the flak fire from a distance of fifty miles. We made our run up to the aiming point from a westerly direction. Owing to the intense flak barrage, we did not actually locate the aiming point but we were certain that we were over the target area. At 0200 hours we dropped 2 x 500lb and 2 x 250lb GP bombs and 2 SBC's incendiaries in a stick east to west. The bomb bursts were not observed but the incendiaries were seen burning. No fires were burning either on our arrival or when we left. The return flight was uneventful and we landed at 0550 hours. *Trip 8 hours 10 minutes*

On my last trip to Dusseldorf, weather conditions were not very good and on return we were called by radio to land at Tangmere which was the only aerodrome free from fog. The whole of Bomber Command landed there that night, and I had just arrived in the Mess at Tangmere when the

Germans started bombing us. In the morning we went out to the aerodrome to fly back to base and discovered the damage. Our plane was undamaged but quite a few planes had been hit and the ones that escaped were sitting in bomb craters. Taxiing in the dark after landing proved difficult as these craters could not be seen, and as it was a grass runway, planes seemed to be at all angles.

Dusseldorf March 15 1941

We left base at 1900 hours and crossed the coast at Aldeburgh at 1939 hours at 5000 feet and flew on track to the target; about halfway between the Dutch coast and the target the navigator saw a line of flares extending about five miles north east to south west which we crossed at right angles. Twenty five search lights were on each side of the flare paths. We were over the target for eight minutes and dropped our bombs at 2127 hours from 10,000 feet. The flak was at times accurate and directed at us. Owing to the haze we could not observe the results of our bombing but after dropping them we saw the palls of white smoke which seemed to be caused by our bombs. We returned on track and again saw the long track of flares among the searchlights. We turned south west at 2247 hours at 10,000 feet and made landfall east of Dungeness. We followed the coast at 2000 feet to Selsey Bill and saw Tangmere beacon at 2350 hours. We landed without difficulty at 0015 hours.

Trip 5 hours 50 minutes

Operations finished and I was posted back to Finningley 25 O.T.V. as a Staff Pilot. We settled all our bills at the bungalow, packed our belongings into the car and set off once more.

Chapter nine

Finningley
April 8 1941 – October 25 1941

We arrived at Finningley and Norah dropped me off at the base, and went on into Doncaster to find some digs. We arranged to meet outside The Elephant at 6pm. This all went to plan and we now had accommodation with a couple called Le Fevre.

Flying at Finningley was confined mainly to taking up navigators and air gunners to do practice bombing, high level and low level, and high level night bombing. The gunners did their air firing at a drogue over Filey Bay in Yorkshire.

One evening I was detailed for ACP (Aerodrome Control Pilot), which consisted of laying out the flare path, and controlling the landing and take-off of aircraft. The flare path was lit by Glim lamps (bulb about the size of a flash lamp) laid out across the landing area in the form of a T. The Chance light which was a very bright landing light, was situated slightly left of the flare path with the light shining down it. This light was switched on at the last minute for the aircraft to touch down, then it was switched off immediately. I was positioned 50 yards to the left of the flare path with the red and green Aldis lamp. On this particular night we had a ground mist, and even flying above the mist the flare path could be seen quite clearly. However, it could not be seen until the last minute if landing at an angle and it became difficult to line up with the flare path.

An aircraft entered the circuit and with its lamp requested permission to land. I gave him a green signal back with the Aldis lamp. It was difficult to see the lights of the aircraft on its final approach due to the mist, when suddenly it flew very low over my head missing the flare path completely. Realising this he opened the throttle and went round for a second try. Again I gave him another green for landing and the same thing happened. On the third attempt I gave him a green and then jumped into a van parked nearby and got well away from the flare path. I could hear the aircraft approaching for its final time when suddenly I heard a crunch and the aircraft burst into flames just inside the boundary of the aerodrome. It had undershot and hit a nissan hut. Within seconds it was a mass of flames and I could just make out the geodetic construction of a Wellington. I jumped back into the van to go to its aid and saw the silhouettes of men walking through the flames – the crew had managed to get out. The fire tender and ambulance were in attendance by now.

When I finished my duty I went into the Mess for supper and to my joy and amazement there was the crew of the Wellington having their supper. I asked after them and they were all without serious injury, even the rear gunner who had to be rescued by the fire crews, and he was only affected by the smoke and fumes.

The only other occasion was when I was stationed at Finningley, and Doncaster wanted to give their emergency services some practice. Myself and another pilot were detached to fly over certain points in the town low level to simulate enemy attack. The points we had to 'attack' at low level were the railway station and police station. This was great fun and we made the most of it. Norah and Joan went to watch this mock raid and Norah borrowed Mrs Le Fevre's identity card as she had lost her own. In Doncaster, they were stopped by a policeman, who asked why they were in a no-go area. Norah attempted to explain that her husband was a pilot and flying overhead, but this did not impress him and he accused them of being spies and demanded to see their identity cards. He then asked Norah what her Christian name was, and as she was in possession of Mrs. Le Fevre's card she could not answer. After much discussion he decided to take them to the police station. Just as they arrived a smoke bomb exploded in the station and to simplify things they were both told to clear off.

The next day the policeman called at our lodgings to return the card and invited Norah to the cinema. She refused and said that it really had been her husband flying overhead the day before.

Chapter ten

RAF Church Lawford – No 2 Central flying School
October 26 1941 – December 19 1941

Flying at Finningly was getting rather tedious and so I applied to do an Instructor's Course. Several months passed before the acceptance came through and I was posted to Church Lawford No 2 Central Flying School on October 26. Once again we loaded all our belongings into the car and set off for Rugby which was the nearest town to Church Lawford. Eventually we found a bungalow to rent.

We started flying from scratch. The aircraft we used were the Avro Tutor and the Airspeed Oxford. We went through the whole syllabus and our flying had to be very accurate. If the Instructor said to climb at 200 feet per minute it had to be precisely that. In fact the realisation dawned on us that we had previously been flying in a rather slovenly manner; literally getting the aircraft into the air and landing again somehow.

Now things were different as we had pupils to instruct. The Tutor was a lovely aircraft to fly. Not having flown singles since elementary, my acrobatics were very shaky but I soon found that if I lost my bearings and the horizon disappeared, I could let go of the control column and take my feet off the rudder and the aircraft would come out in a gentle dive.

We were at Church Lawford until December 19 1941 and I was then posted to RAF Pembrey. This was a mistake and when it was sorted out I was moved to AFU(O) Advanced Flying Unit (Observers) Wigtown on January 6 1942. By now Norah had joined the WAAFS as a telephone operator. As husband and wife we expected to be posted together, but I was sent to Wigtown, Scotland and Norah to Heyford (Oxfordshire) and this was as near as we ever got to one another.

Chapter eleven

Wigtown
January 6 1942 – 11 May 1942

It was while I was at Wigtown that a new regulation was announced. Up until then it had been impossible for Sergeant Pilots to be promoted and now that ruling had been overturned. I became a Flight Sergeant backdated to April 1941, and a Warrant Officer in January 1942 all in the same week! The Warrant Officer was one of the best ranks in the Air Force and received respect from airmen and officers alike.

The aircraft I was flying now were the Anson, Blenheim Mk1, Blenheim Mk IV and Lysander. Not having flown the Blenheims or Lysanders before, I had to pass out before I was qualified to instruct on them. My particular job on this station was to instruct any new pilot in the particular aircraft in which he was to fly, and check him out day and night.

The staff pilots would fly them around for their exercises. When all the pilots were qualified on their own types of aircraft, I had finished my job. A wireless operator airgunner named Bell, otherwise called Dinger, on the staff also had very little to do at times and so we would take a Lysander for a joy ride over the mountains. We really enjoyed ourselves, although one danger was a particular mountain 2331 feet high called Cairnsmore of Fleet. This mountain was in line with the main runway ten miles away, and it had claimed five lives from Wigtown out of the twenty three, who had lost their lives in the mountains. One of our aircraft went missing and although the whole station went in search over the moors, it was never found.

Here at Wigtown we had snow and the Station Snow Plan was put into operation which meant that the whole station turned out to sweep the runway. Dinger Bell and myself did not think much of this but we had to do it. Anyway it snowed a second time and we decided to get snowed up out of camp. We walked up the railway line to Newton Stewart and stayed in a hotel until the road was clear. We caught the bus back again and it broke down on the journey. I removed the autovac (sort of petrol pump) and I can't remember what I did next, but we got back to the base ok.

I stayed here until May 11 and was then posted to No 1 Staff Pilots Training Unit (No.1 SPTU) at Cark near Cartmel in Lancashire, south of Grange over Sands. Again, my first pupil who was a Canadian, went through the far hedge at the end of the runway on his first solo – so much for my instruction!

Airspeed Oxford

Blenheim

Lysander

Chapter twelve

Cartmel
May 11 1942 – September 11 1942

Norah was expecting our first child and so left the WAAFS. I found us lodgings in a village called Cartmel, about four miles from Cark. I had a service bicycle and cycled daily to and from the station. Norah would come and meet me in the evenings and I would give her a lift back on the bar of the bicycle. Most evenings were spent in the Kings Arms, Cartmel round the piano.

Before moving to Cartmel, Norah lived in Worcester with her parents. One day the CO went off for the day. The Flight Commander decided to take an Anson to the Isle of Man for the day, so when they had both gone I shouted to the other lads 'Anyone for down south?' So we took an Anson and I dropped one chap off at Bobbington, Nr Wolverhampton, and another at Rissington arranging times to meet them later. I then went on to Worcester and had tea with Norah. Worcester was a very small aerodrome, very tight for landing and taking off, but all was well. We finally bade our goodbyes and set off on the journey back to base, picking up the other two, and arriving safely later that evening. No one ever knew about it. Not so easy these days!

This was the station where we met Tiny Cooling and Joan his wife, and we became lifelong friends. We all lived fairly near Lake Windermere and we would cycle to Newby Bridge, go to the pub in the evenings, about three miles away, and sometimes take a boat out on Lake Windermere.

Chapter thirteen

Dumfries
September 11 1942 – November 7 1942

On September 11 I was posted to 10 O.A.F.U. Dumfries, the Observer Advanced Flying Unit. There I was back as a Staff Pilot flying Ansons for the Observers to practice low level bombing and the odd cross country. When the weather was unfit for flying the Flight Commander would take us down to Dumfries to a pub for a session. This was allowed when the weather was bad, but on one occasion during a session, the weather cleared and we had to rush back and start flying. Not too clever when you've had a few!

On November 7 1942 I was posted to Kirmington; this was a mistake and while the powers that be were sorting out the muddle, I had very little to do as a Warrant Officer. I had to take the Station Parade and hand over to the adjutant now and again, and the Station Commander on one occasion. Apart from this I had nothing to do except wait for news from Norah. At last it came and Jonathan was born on November 17. Toys were not very plentiful but I managed to buy a little monkey; it was not really a suitable present for a new-born baby, but it was the only thing available. We were both pleased that everything had gone well, especially Norah who had someone to comfort and cuddle. I could not leave base so I didn't see Jonathan for three weeks.

Then at last my posting came for Kemble.

Chapter fourteen

Kemble – January 17 1943 – November 30 1943

I was posted to RAF Kemble on January 17 1943 as a Test Pilot. It was called O.A.P.U. Overseas Aircraft Preparation Unit. The aircraft were given special modifications for flying overseas eg desert. We would test the aircraft when delivered by the Air Transport Auxillary from the factory. They would then go through the workshops and we would give them an hour's test when they came out. Crews would pick them up from us and fly them straight out to the desert via Gibralter.

This was an interesting job as it entailed flying all types of aircraft that came in. The pilot would have to sit in the aircraft with the pilot's notes for that particular type to become familiar with the exact position of the different controls, and then once you had memorised them, flying was as easy as riding a bicycle. The main reactions by the rudder and control column were the same in all aircraft but some had a few nasty tendencies, so we had to be quick to spot any vices the aircraft had, like a violent swing on take-off and landing etc. The majority of our aircraft came straight from the factories and I accepted one from Jim Mollinson, who was in the Air Transport Auxillary, and then had to give it an acceptance test, to look for any faults to report before going into the workshops.

The aircraft were mainly multi engine and twins, Wellingtons, Hudsons, Mosquitos, Halifax, Beaufighters and Bostons – not forgetting the C.O.'s Leopard Moth. Kemble was a small unit with about six pilots, six wireless operators and air gunners. Flying was carried out between 9am and 5pm.

When things got quiet I would get the ground staff to push out the C.O.'s Leopard Moth and trip over to Worcester to see Norah and Jonathan. This was unofficial, but not difficult to do in such a small unit. Life at Kemble was very pleasant. The Sergeants Mess was situated in Kemble House, a large country house set in beautiful grounds. The house had large windows and one particular night, one of the lads, Jock Gallie, having been out on the beer, walked out of a first floor window thinking he was on the ground floor, escaping only with a broken arm.

By this time, I managed to find some digs for Norah and Jonathan, now six months old, on a farm opposite the Sergeants Mess. I had just been commissioned and was now a Pilot Officer and now instead of cycling to and from the airfield, transport was sent to pick me up, which was luxurious!

As a new officer I had to eat in the Officers Mess once a month and learn the necessary etiquette. The CO was a Wing Commander Stocken, a very pleasant chap and easy to get on with.

While I was living out at Kemble I had a temporary posting to 4 O.A.P.U. Melton Mowbray, doing the same work and also flying Beaufighters. The maintenance on this unit was poor, and aircraft were giving a lot of trouble and the pilots were losing confidence. I did not trust the ground staff to do their job properly. After six weeks I came back to Kemble for a weekend. A friend, named Nick Carter, who was single, swapped places with me and a week later he was killed.

Suddenly a posting to RCAF Station Patricia Bay, BC Canada came through. Norah went back to live with her parents in Worcester and just before I left I approached the CO and asked his permission to borrow the

Leopard Moth to fly to Worcester and say my goodbyes to Norah and Jonathan. He agreed to this and all was above board this time, and he was sorry to hear of my posting.

	DIS
MAGISTER	63.00
OXFORD	176.50
TUTOR	19.35
HAMPDEN	451.35
WELLINGTON	344.35
ANSON	236.55
T. MOTH	5.00
HEREFORD	20.35
BLENHEIM	10.05
LYSANDER	5.00
MASTER	.50
HUDSON	59.45
MOSQUITO	15.25
HALIFAX	45.30
L MOTH	6.10
BOSTON	.30
BEAUFIGHTER	4.45
DAKOTA	395.25
EXPEDITOR	252.45
	2116.15

Total flying hours in each aircraft

Chapter fifteen

Canada – Patricia Bay

We left Kemble on November 30 1943 and assembled at Blackpool No.5 PDC. It was here that I met Ted Sanderson who was also posted to Patricia Bay. We stayed in a boarding house in Blackpool with four other chaps. Patricia Bay was an OTU flying Hampdens – so I expect that was the reason I was sent there. One day at Blackpool Ted Sanderson (Sandy) and I had an unexpected job to do. The police called at our boarding house and told us that one of the chaps living in the boarding house with us had committed suicide, and we had to identify him in the mortuary. He was not one of our close friends, but this was a sad and disturbing event.

We were at Blackpool for about one week getting our kit sorted out for the voyage ahead. Then news arrived that we were to report to Greenock. We left Blackpool with a few uninteresting sandwiches and arrived at Greenock at 6am cold, weary, and fed up with the prospect of leaving England.

One other chap, Pete Ludlow, joined Sandy and I as we waited on the dockside for it to get light, and gradually we could see the outline of the ship. It was the QE2. We were kept on the shore for ages and later found out that the Customs men had gone on board for breakfast. There was no rationing in the U.S. and the ship had been stocked up with food in the U.S. so they didn't want to miss out on a good meal.

Arriving on the ship we were allocated our cabins, Sandy, Pete and myself in one cabin, then on to the dining room for breakfast. This was truly luxurious, six to a table and three waiters to a table. We had been on rationing in England for a long time and could not believe our eyes when we saw ham and eggs on the menu, and 'seconds' as well which we all took advantage of. We were fortunate in one respect in going from East to West, because the ship was not overcrowded and we had ample room. West to East was a different matter and G.I.'s were sleeping three to a bed, eight hours each – so the beds never got cold. James Cagney was travelling on the ship with us and entertained us all one evening at a concert.

We did a zig zag course across the Atlantic to avoid U boats. The first leg was a northerly course and it got very cold, then southerly, eventually another northerly course into New York harbour. Passing the Statue of Liberty we changed our money with the help of the waiters and decided to go 'missing' in New York until our money ran out. But the people in charge were extremely well organised and put a stop to that. Straight off the boat, on to a train and we were on our way to Canada. I remember the excellent food on the train – such a contrast to food in England.

We arrived at Moncton, New Brunswick which was a centre where all postings to Canada were assembled before going on to final destinations. While we were there, after a session in the bar, Sandy took down a fire axe (fire axes were hanging from all walls as the buildings were wooden) and went down to the town. We went into a Chinese restaurant for a meal, and the poor little proprietor spotting Sandy with his villainous black moustache and fire axe rang the police and Sandy was arrested. He spent the night in jail and a few of us had to club together to pay his fine and get him out the next day.

From Moncton, Pete, Sandy and I travelled on to Ottowa and at the RCAF's expense stayed at the Elgin Hotel, which was large and sumptuous. We were given the choice of a trip across Canada with either the Canadian National Railway or Canadian Pacific Railway. We were advised to go CPR so we settled for that, and while in Ottawa I arranged to send some food parcels home to Norah. By paying a lump sum you could choose what you wanted to send, and they would send one parcel a month. These were very much appreciated by Norah because she was receiving food she hadn't seen for years.

The trip across Canada took four nights, five days. Once again super food with lots of fresh salmon. The journey seemed to take ages crossing the prairies, mile after mile of fairly flat land dotted with the occasional farm. The scenery started to change at Calgary and the foothills of the Rockies were now in sight. From now on until our arrival in Vancouver the scenery was spectacular, following rivers through passes and gullies and canyons and through spiral tunnels. These were a way of getting to a lower level – a tunnel leading into a mountain and descending in a half circle which came out at a lower level. The scenery was breathtaking and never to be forgotten. Over the Great Divide through Kicking Horse Canyon was a fantastic trip.

We were given meal tickets for the journey in Ottowa, so enjoyed excellent food, and even our beds were made by the porter on the train. We were living in luxury at the Government's expense.

We eventually arrived in Vancouver where we boarded a ferry for Patricia Bay on Vancouver Island (which is now Victoria's airport). The ferry weaved its way past the island and after about two hours we arrived in Victoria. From there we had transport to Patricia Bay.

We were not here very long. The Hampdens had gone and the unit had moved on to Comox about halfway up the island flying Beechcraft C45's and Dakotas C47's. We stayed at Patricia Bay as long as we could and explored Victoria. This was a very British town and a number of Britons had retired there. Cricket is played there and afternoon tea served at the Empress Hotel, even to this day. When our money was exhausted we had to make a move to Comox some 150 miles away. This was done by ferry from Victoria to Nanaimo and then bus to Courtenay and Comox. Sandy was a Flying Officer, I was a Pilot Officer and Pete Ludlow a Warrant Officer but Pete applied for his commission and was soon to join us.

Comox was a Transport Command OTU. Pupils were mainly instructors from the Canadian Flying Schools, which at this time were closing down. They would be converted to Beechcraft and Dakotas and eventually pass out as Transport Pilots. Before this could be done we had also to be converted to the types, as we three had not flown them before.

Vancouver Island is about 300 miles long and Comox is situated about half-way up on the east side, looking across the sea to the Rockies, and to the west were the mountains rising up to seven thousand feet. So we were between the two, which meant that our safety height in bad weather was critical.

Canadian aircraft were fitted with American radio range, which was essential for getting down in bad weather. Radio range stations were situated at intervals on the east coast of America and Canada and their beams north and south made Airway No.1 up the whole country as far as Alaska and south to California. The pilot had two radios to tune in with, one would be tuned to the next station and the other tuned to the station just passed at the rear – so we were always in touch with one of them. The idea was to stay on course, a steady note (the beam). If we wandered to the left an A or N signal would be heard and the same would happen if we wandered to the right, so an alteration of course would put you back on the beam on a steady note. We also had a radio compass, which could be switched on and it would point to any station tuned into.

Sandy and I were in the same flight and shared the same room in the Officers Quarters. We were each given four pupils, two for the morning and two for the afternoon. A chart on the wall kept a record of hours flown by each pupil and coloured red for solo and blue for dual.

It was May 30 when we arrived in Comox and we had sunshine until the end of September. This was followed by a wet winter with snow on Christmas Day and Boxing Day only. We were starting to know our way around after a few weeks and with its drinking laws we found that it was illegal to carry a bottle of hard liquor (whisky, gin etc) with the seal broken, and drinking was not allowed in public. There were beer parlours in Courtenay, men in one room and ladies in the other, and we had to be seated. Beer was rationed and we were allowed two dozen beers, or one bottle of whisky per month. The beer parlours would put up a notice saying maybe open 5–7pm, so it was a fight to get a drink and the local loggers would come in and have their fill.

There was a golf club at Comox and a Scotsman ran it. He would fix us up with clubs etc .and we started playing quite often. This was the reason that Sandy's and my pupils had a lot of red marked solo hours on the chart. We would send them off in the afternoon for two hours radio range and we would go off for our golf.

We met a local chap called Filberg, a millionaire and he used to take us fishing. He was doing very well selling spruce for building the Mosquitos in England. We went with two cars and two trailers carrying boats into the mountains for trout fishing. It was too easy. The fish would take any fly, blue or brown, wet or dry. One day we caught 120 fish in a very short time and then went back to the house for a fry-up. He invited us for Christmas dinner, which we ate at about midnight. We had trips to logging camps and sawmills, and actually celebrated the end of the war in his house.

The house is now called Filberg Lodge and Park. It was given to the town of Comox – designated a heritage site and opened to the public – there is also Filberg Museum.

Flying and training were still proceeding after the war with Germany was over, so Sandy and I, to get home to England, volunteered to go on the course we were instructing in. This we managed to do, and as we had been instructors had very little to do.

Chapter sixteen

Going Home – May 26 1945

At last we were posted back to England on May 26 1945. We travelled through the Rockies again and back to Moncton to wait for a ship. On June 12 1945 we boarded the Louis Pasteur which brought us back to Southampton arriving on June 17 1945. We were all sent to another holding centre at Morecombe, and from there posted to 525 Squadron at Membury, a transport squadron ferrying army personnel back from India. After some local flying day and night, it was decided to take about fourteen pilots to show them the route for India and return.

After being kitted up with khaki uniform we took off on August 9 with a Wing Commander Dennison to first stop Elmas on the island of Sardinia. We then flew to El Adam in the North African desert and this was a night flight; from El Adam to Lydda in Palestine by day and from Lydda to Habbaniya at night.

While we were at Lydda I thought it a good idea to telephone my brother John, who was stationed at Ramat David further north. John, also in the RAF, was stationed in the Middle East for the whole of the war. I managed to make contact with him and I asked him to make his way to Lydda in about seven days, and we could take him home. But that night I was taken ill with 'gippo gut' (dysentery). I reported sick at around midnight but I was informed that they could do nothing for me until the morning and to report again then. The aircraft was due to take off at 2 am for Habbaniya so they made me a bed on the floor of the aircraft and I reported sick there. I was in sick quarters for about five days during which we heard about the atom bomb in Japan. We all thought we were destined for the Far East eventually, but the bomb stopped the war immediately, and must have saved many thousands of our lives. While I was sick in Habbaniya the aircraft went on and left me behind. I was told to get back the best way I could. I spent a couple of days there before I had the chance of a lift in another of our squadron's aircraft.

Habbaniya was a very large base with English trees and English birds especially imported, and the road was lined with eucalyptus trees. The British Government also had its base there. There was an open air cinema and two swimming pools. The weather was hot, but it was a dry heat and bearable. The Mess was luxurious and we were waited on at the meal table, by three very tall Iraqi waiters, all dressed in long white robes with RAF buttons, and with wide RAF sashes around their waists – and of course topped by the red fez. There were three waiters again to a table of six. A very young Iraqi boy sat behind the bar, aged about thirteen/fourteen and when we ordered drinks we could pay in any currency. When we checked our change, which took considerable time because of the mixture of coins, we found that he was never wrong. Very difficult to do.

A few traders used to come to the base from Basra to sell their wares, mainly silver items and I bought a silver snake bangle for Norah.

The time came to move and one of our squadron was on a return flight to the UK; I had my lift home via Almaza (Cairo) Castel Benito, Tripoli and then on to England. Meanwhile my brother John, had gone down to Lydda but owing to the delay by me going sick, was out of luck.

Sandy, acquired a great dislike for mountains in Canada, but ended up by flying The Hump, mountains between Burma and China. I didn't envy him. The Dakota could just struggle over the top without much to spare.

My second trip to India was more successful. The first leg was to Elmas on the island of Sardinia. Our crew disembarked, the aircraft refuelled and a fresh crew boarded and carried on. This way the aircraft kept moving but as fresh crews were flying different aircraft, the aircraft snags were not reported. We picked up our next aircraft two days later and flew it to El Adam (North Africa) at night. This was when I met up with Sandy and heard all about him flying The Hump. We refuelled and then went on to Lydda in Palestine, then on to Habbaniya and then on to Bahrain.

Bahrain was very hot with high humidity and within seconds of landing our shirts were sticking to us. They were in the process of fitting air conditioning in the buildings, and the foreman who lodged in the Sergeants Mess fitted the Sergeants Mess out first, naturally. So I took off my badges of rank and booked in as a Sergeant to get a decent night's sleep. Without air conditioning, the nights were unbearable; we would lie on top of our beds mopping the perspiration with a towel, and the mosquito nets seemed to trap the heat in. During the day we sat in the swimming pool up to our necks but were not allowed to put our heads under for fear of throat or ear infection. The pool, by the way, was just a large water tank.

Drinking water was the colour of tea and the strong taste of it could not be disguised by anything else, which wasn't helped by putting us on American K rations, which was a small box containing biscuits, chocolate and other thirst making foods.

We were not sorry to leave Bahrain for Mauripur, which is the airport for Karachi. One night's stop here, and then on to Poonah. We were supposed to fly to Poonah and return the same day, but we stayed the night and went round the town the next day looking for bargains. The snag with these trips was that we were always short of money. The first thing we did at a staging post was to go to the accounts section and try to draw some of our pay. We also usually had the wrong money for the country we were in. We were always changing money en route and ended up in Karachi with lira, mils, fils, dinars and rupees etc.

Before leaving Karachi we went down into the town; carpets and rugs were in great demand at home so each of the crew bought what they could afford in the way of floor coverings either for themselves, or to sell. Carpets and rugs were in very short supply at home. I remember the poverty in Karachi, people sleeping on the pavements, sacred cows wandering across the streets, a dead goat which had been run over, people gathering the dung from the cows making it into fuel bricks when dried in the sun, and children pestering you to buy something, red patches on the pavements and walls where they spit after chewing beetlenuts.

So the passengers had been waiting and they were anxious to get back to the UK. So back to Bahrain and on to Shaibah, missing Habbaniya on a night trip, more to pick up and then on to Lydda and El Adam. After leaving El Adam for Elmas we developed some trouble with an engine so I put in at Luqa in Malta to be checked. After a test flight it was still giving trouble so I returned to Luqa. At the time the passengers, who consisted of Colonels, Majors and Privates, were trying to make me press on, but as I was the Captain of the aircraft there was not much they could do about it. Eventually we arrived safely at Membury. We had been away nearly three weeks.

One week's leave, and then a repeat trip on the same route. In Palestine we took a trip into the nearest town – Tel Aviv. The terrorists were very active against the British, and when we arrived there had just been an explosion in a shop, and although we wanted to go and look we were advised against it. So our stay was a short one. Back in Karachi the dead goat was still in the road, but much flatter!

Demobilisation had just begun and my demob number was 22 group, and I listened intently to the news to see how near they were getting to my number. Twenty one groups went and so I thought if I could take my time on this trip, I should be right for demob when I arrived back. More carpets were bought in Karachi and the return trip completed. By this time the customs were very active at base and would drive a van out to a returning aircraft to check. On landing I would taxi as fast as possible to the far side of the aerodrome, open the door, throw the carpets out and then pick them up later when it was dark. This worked for me at the time, but I think they tumbled to it later.

At last 22 group was due for demob. The CO said at first that they were keeping 22 group on and releasing them later. I told him that I had a job and a house to go to, and so he relented and kept back 23 group instead.

On November 6 1945 I was posted to 100 PDC Uxbridge for demob and to be fitted out with civilian clothes. Asked if I would like an aircraft to take me, I declined and took a rail warrant. It was many years later before I could bring myself to board an aircraft again. I took the train back to my wife and child and looked forward to living a normal life.

BOMBER COMMAND LOST 56,000 MEN AND WOMEN

BOMBER COMMAND LOST 8953 AIRCRAFT

144 SQUADRON 2045 SORTIES 62 LOST

HAMPDENS 15,771 SORTIES 417 LOST

AERODROMES I LANDED AT DURING WAR 39–45

1. Kidlington
2. Marham
3. Conningsby
4. Warwick
5. Cambridge
6. Bircham Newton
7. Brough
8. Church Lawford
9. Montrose
10. Weston Super Mare
11. Brockworth
12. Sibson
13. Kinloss
14. Tangmere
15. Lossiemouth
16. Skellingthorpe
17. Heyford
18. St Eval
19. Desford
20. Wigtown
21. Ternhill
22. Boscombe Down
23. Kemble
24. Cark
25. Shawbury
26. South Cerney
27. Honnington
28. Ayre
29. Finningley
30. Lindholme
31. Cheltenham
32. Millom
33. Hemswell
34. Sealand
35. Cottam
36. Bobbington
37. Scampton
38. Cranfield
39. Swinderby
40. Worcester
41. Waddington
42. Cottesmore
43. Driffield
44. Cranwell
45. Edzel
46. Brackley
47. Ingham
48. Jurby
49. Walney Island
50. Dumfries
51. Hawarden
52. Staverton
53. Kirmington
54. Lyneham
55. Castle Bromwich
56. Alconbury
57. Aston Down
58. Atherstone
59. StAthens
60. White Waltham
61. Shellingford
62. Llandow
63. Whitchurch
64. Moreton in Marsh
65. Defford
66. Tempsford
67. Bramcote
68. Pershore
69. Hendon
70. Watchfield
71. Woofax Lodge
72. Melton Mowbray
73. Docking
74. Filton
75. Colerne
76. Comox, BC Canada
77. Patricia Bay, BC Canada
78. Sea Island, Vancouver, BC Canada
79. Tofina, BC Canada
80. Port Hardy, BC Canada
81. Sand Point, Seattle USA
82. Membury
83. Prestwick
84. Elmas, Sardinia
85. El Adam, North Africa
86. Lydda, Palestine
87. Habbaniya, Iraq
88. Almaza, Cairo
89. Castel Benito, Tripoli
90. Bahrein, Persian Gulf
91. Mauripur, India
92. Poona, India
93. Shaibah, Iraq
94. Luqa, Malta
95. Blyton
96. Merryfield

AIRCRAFT FLOWN

S – Single engine   T – Twin engine   M – Multi engine

De Haviland	Miles Magister	S	Gypsy Major
De Haviland	Tiger Moth	S	Gypsy III
Avro	Tutor	S	Lynx
Airspeed	Oxford	T	Cheetah X
Avro	Anson	T	Cheetah IX
Handley Page	Hereford	T	Napier Dagger
Handley Page	Hampden	T	Pegasus XVIII
Vickers	Wellington Mk 1A	T	Pegasus XVIII
Vickers	Wellington Mk1C	T	Pegasus XVIII
Vickers	Wellington Mk II	T	Merlin X
Vickers	Wellington Mk III	T	Hercules XI
Vickers	Wellington Mk DWI	T	Pegasus XVIII
Vickers	Wellington Mk X	T	Hercules VI
Vickers	Wellington Mk XI	T	Hercules VI
Vickers	Wellington Mk XII	T	Hercules VI
Vickers	Wellington Mk XIII	T	Hercules XVII
Vickers	Wellington Mk XIV	T	Hercules XVII
Vickers	Wellington Mk VIII	T	Pegasus XVIII
Bristol	Blenheim Mk 1	T	Mercury
Bristol	Blenheim Mk IV	T	Mercury
Westland	Lysander	S	Perseus
Miles	Master	S	Pratt-Whitney
Lockheed	Hudson Mk VI	T	Twin Wasp
Lockheed	Hudson Mk V	T	Wright Cyclone
De Haviland	Leopard Moth	S	Gypsy Major
De Haviland	Mosquito Mk VI	T	Merlin XXIII
De Haviland	Halifax Mk II	M	Merlin XX
Douglas	Boston Mk III	T	Double Cyclone
Handley Page	Halifax Mk V	M	Merlin
Lockheed	Hudson Mk III	T	Cyclone
Handley Page	Halifax Mk II	M	Merlin
Lockheed	Hudson Mk IV	T	Cyclone
Bristol	Beaufighter Mk X	T	Hercules XVII
Beechcraft	Expeditor C45	T	Wasp Junior
Douglas	Dakota C47	T	Twin Wasp
Handley Page	Halifax III	M	Hercules XVI

Chapter seventeen

2005
Norah's Story

Since Bob died, I spend a lot of my time at Bob's desk, it's actually my favourite place to be. I am not waiting for inspiration, I know that when I have to do that, it won't come, so all that I write is right to share. I shall only write about incidents. I hope they connect, but most important I hope the reading of this will make clear the truth of the days we shared during the war years, to tell of the love we shared, of the hopes we had, and of the fun we had too.

Bob and I met and became good friends in 1939. It seemed as if I had lived in a cocoon all my life which had been so sheltered, then suddenly applying for, and getting, (my parents being so proud) a post at Elliston & Cavells, Oxford, and leaving home for the first time. It seemed a sunny adventure, my father taking me for my interview. I remember the journey through Burford being so exciting, now I know why. I had always dreamed that I would meet a boy who lived half way up a hill on the right hand side and we would become friends.

I didn't connect my dream to reality, but I know this was God's plan for us. He watched over us, blessing us all the way. Bob lived half way up the hill in Burford (on the right hand side) in a house called Hill View, and I was to meet this special person very soon.

Chapter eighteen

My sister and I had a fairly uneventful time growing up. We led sheltered, happy and very nurtured lives. I was born in Worcester in 1918, just before the end of the First World War. My father was an army ambulance driver in the Great War, serving in the trenches until the end of the war. He was gassed, and had shrapnel in his legs and when he returned home he had to strip in the garden, before he could come into the house, to be cleansed. He had his hair shaved off also and this carried on fortnightly throughout his life, a bone of contention for our mother. He drank so heavily the following year that the doctor told him that he if continued for another year he would not be alive, and just like him, he stopped drinking not touching any alcohol for the rest of his life (not even a sherry trifle). He was very strong-minded, and very patriotic. We had to always stand for the National Anthem, which was played very regularly on the radio. I do remember always feeling that thrill of patriotism. Dad taught me to read before I went to school at four years old.

Our mother was patient, loving and very good with us all. Ethel, my sister, is like her in many ways. We had musical evenings, mainly on Tuesdays when we sang round the piano. Our mother was a pianist and had a friend who joined us in the singing. She, Clarice, had a lovely voice, and we all trilled away together.

We went to our first school, a little private school quite near home and pedalled there and back on our fairy cycles. Apparently our parents were not happy with our progress and found another school called Red Hill School on the other side of Worcester. We had to travel on trams, first into the centre of Worcester, and the second up to Red Hill, quite a journey for two youngsters. Then we went on to a secondary school, a girls' grammar school.

I left school at 18 years old and had the idea of being a dress designer, and found an apprenticeship in a Gown Salon in Malvern. I had two lovely years there, holding pin cushions for dress makers, and modelling a little for customers. I remember talking to the artist Dame Laura Knight. Then the time came for my apprenticeship to end. I was almost 21 years old. I wrote away answering an advertisement for the position of buyer in the mantle department of Elliston and Cavell, rather a grand establishment in Oxford. I had no idea how presumptuous it was to apply for the post of buyer as I had no experience, but I received a reply and an appointment for an interview.

I couldn't bring myself to tell my parents that I was about to leave home so I wrote a letter to them, thanking them for everything and telling them of the interview, and pushed it under their bedroom door. My father came to me and told me that they were proud of me and that he would take me for the interview. Matters proceeded quickly, and although the post I applied for I didn't get because I was too young, I was offered another, and there I was working in the same establishment as Bob, and so it goes.

Oxford was so beautiful then and there was lots to enjoy, the theatre (6d up 'in the gods'), punting on the river etc. I enjoyed too, the work in the mantle department of Elliston & Cavell. I lived with other girls working there in a hostel in Keble Road, opposite Keble College. I used to read a lot in the nearby park, and I became friendly with an undergraduate called Bill (Horsley). We met travelling on the train to Worcester, and we went about together. We enjoyed tea in the college, boating and the theatre.

I rarely saw the window dressers and had hardly spoken to Bob. I found out later that the others teased him about me, and they found out that Bill used to meet me after work. Anyway one day Bob suddenly asked me if I would like to see his car, and I thought this was kind of him so I said yes. I was pleased to be asked though I had no idea he liked me. We met up, and Bob being shy, asked two friends to come with us for a drive in this tiny very ancient car, which he was extremely proud of. The most exciting moment of my life was when he took my hand to hold it. I cannot explain fully how this tiny loving gesture changed my life.

From then on life changed drastically. I said farewell to Bill, and began to know the responsibility of loving someone. I suppose that was when I started to grow up. The war loomed very strongly around our dreams.

Chapter nineteen

It was a lovely dreamlike summer. We had fun sharing the simplest pleasures for neither of us had a lot of cash. As the summer passed the clouds of war became threatening, though most of us young people seemed unaffected by this, and enjoyed ourselves all the more. It was strange because we were aware that this heavenly summer would end soon.

The night before war was declared, a group of us went to a small village hop in Fairford. As we travelled back home to Burford it started thundering and lightening, and I remember seeming to know the good times of peace were at an end.

On September 3, a Sunday, we all listened with sinking hearts to the radio hearing the words 'this country is at war with Germany' and each one present had their fears. I believe my mother in law must have been the bravest and saddest there, though I could only think of my own great heartache, that of losing, even temporarily the young man I had grown to love. We all held one another and suddenly that day was over and the war had begun. We shared as much time together as we could, and in the September just before Bob was posted, he opened what he called his bottom drawer and took all his savings, about six pounds ten shillings and bought me the sweetest little engagement ring.

We began by not being able to see a future, and the thoughts of a home and being together seemed too good to ever be true. Suddenly everything changed around us. Bob was called up and was straightway made an RAF Sergeant Pilot, because he was already in the

RAF Volunteer Reserves and learning to fly. There I was receiving letters from Bob, now in Bexhill, meeting up occasionally in Burford, until he was posted to Montrose in December 1939. Bob used to write a lot of letters from Montrose, although letters were censored and writing tended to be guarded and restricted.

Letters travelled backwards and forwards each summoning up as much news as possible. Bob had much more to relate. I was still at home with my family in Worcester after a short spell in the Land Army, which involved lots of tractor training on a large farm at Brize Norton. I became ill and my parents came and fetched me home. Bob's letters became more and more the order of the day.

The summer arrived and Bob was posted to Upper Heyford in May 1940. We saw as much of one another as we could. I stayed in Oxford with an aunt, and sometimes in Charlbury with a friend called Paddy. They were good times when we were together, but very scary not knowing what tomorrow would bring, or where he would be posted to next. Suddenly he was posted to a bomber squadron in Hemswell August 1940. He was in action.

Chapter twenty

One day Bob rang my home in Worcester and asked my father's permission to marry me in two weeks, as he had 48 hours leave due. No time, but we managed to get the banns read and wedding date fixed for the 11 November (1940).

Bob baled out of his aircraft returning from Munich three nights before the wedding. He was lame and had to hitchhike to Worcester. We were married at St Johns Church, Worcester at 9.30 am in the morning of November 11 1940 with seven friends and family present. It was pouring with rain. We had a celebration at my home with a handful of family and friends. It poured with rain all day and we were taken by a friend to Nottingham. Bob had to catch a train at 7am the next morning to return to base next day. What a farewell – on a foggy cold dark November morning, both so sad and holding so tightly, as if forever, our friends in the corner sharing our tears. Then we had to part and I found my way back to Worcester. I remember sitting in the train with a little old lady and told her that I was just married and she asked if she could touch me, because she had never been so near to a new bride. Bob and I didn't see each other again until January when we had a week together in Oban.

PEARMAN—GODSALL.—On November 11, at St. John's Church, by the Rev. Rowe, Robert Harvey (Sergt. Pilot, R.A.F.), youngest son of Mrs. H. Pearman, of Burford, Oxon., to Norah Mary, eldest daughter of Mr. and Mrs. H. H. Godsall, of 173, Malvern Road, Worcester.

A WORCESTER WEDDING

The wedding was solemnised at St. John's Church of Miss Norah Mary Godsall, eldest daughter of Mr. and Mrs. Godsall, 173, Malvern-road, Worcester, and Sergeant-Pilot Robert Harvey Pearman, of Burford, Oxford.

The bridegroom was on 48 hours' leave from the R.A.F.

The bride, who was given away by her father, wore a charming two-piece of pale blue and a brown hat trimmed with veiling. She carried a bouquet of pink carnations. Her sister, who acted as maid of honour, wore a two-piece in brown with a spray of pink carnations.

Mr. Robert Hughes, of Kidderminster, was best man.

The Rev. C. Rowe, of Powick, officiated. There was a reception at the bride's home.

Chapter twenty-one

Bob and Ossie, another pilot, found a bungalow called Winfrith in a tiny village called Walesby about 15 miles from Hemswell base so that wives could join them. In January 1941 Joan, Ossie's wife and I travelled from Worcester to Walesby, a village near Market Rasen in Lincolnshire, fifteen miles from the airfield in Bob's Triumph 9. It had no working foot brake, no windscreen wipers, and no indicators. I drove to Kidderminster to pick up Joan and we travelled to Walesby, (no road signs) in a day. It was icy and snowing and we had to be pushed out of several snow drifts. However, we arrived safely.

I vividly remember hearing the planes taking off all through our stay in Lincolnshire. The flat countryside seemed filled with the sound of aircraft, leaving … flying into the unknown darkness. Just imagine the fears of those brave men as they set off on each nightmare flight.

Bob and Ossie would speak to us over the short wave on the radio, and could let us know their flights, or rather the times we could roughly expect them back. The plane would circle the bungalow and we would run in to find the right setting on short wave on the radio and hear them call 'Hello Winfrith' and then give us the information.

One night they told us to expect them at 2am. By 6am in the morning they had not arrived back. We went to the phone box in the village for news – it always amazed me how easy it was to find out what had happened. Ossie had been guided down by Spitfires because his navigation had failed, and Bob had baled out over Norfolk. A lasting memory and one that brings a lump to my throat even now, was the look of them, after a night's bombing, they looked like old men. The flying never left us, even in the times off; there seemed no other life even though we

After baling out

76

never talked about it. The dread was always there, sometimes it seemed as if all the days were night.

Then Ossie was posted on to Finningley, Doncaster, as he had finished his tour of operations. We were on our own for a few weeks, then came Bob's posting. He came home one evening 'tomorrow my posting, no more ops' he said. We were over the moon and couldn't believe this nightmare had come to an end.

The next evening came 6pm and no Bob, so I rang the camp. You could always speak to one another – I shall never forget his words. 'Sorry chick, but I've got one more, the last I promise you', then the longest night ever. He didn't return – I spent the night waiting 4am, 5am, 6am and I rang the camp almost gibbering at 7am. 'Sorry Mrs Pearman, but your husband had to land at Tangmere because of fog. There was an air raid, but he is safe!'

Chapter twenty-two

In April 1941 we moved to Doncaster, and life seemed simple; the occasional dance and fun together. Ossie and Joan were already there, and they were good days. We went horse riding, once only, because my horse took off! I worked in a canteen for servicemen and women and drove a mobile canteen into the wilds to reach a few outposts. The queues for cigarettes and the sparse goodies we took around were always waiting for us.

One day Finningley planned a mock air raid – Bob was asked to fly one of the two planes taking part. Joan and I decided to go down into the town to see the fun. As usual I couldn't find my identity card and borrowed my landlady, Mrs Le Fevres' card, not noting her christian name or her age, and off we went. We got caught in an area we shouldn't have been in, and we were taken by a warden officer to the police station. He questioned me about my age and christian name and of course I didn't know the answers. He concluded that we must be 'mock' German spies and took us to the Police Station which was being 'mock' bombed and the home guard let us go. The next day, he came to return the identity card and had a cup of tea with us. He asked if I would go to the pictures with him, but I said no, that it really had been my husband flying the plane the previous night.

We were happy staying with Mr & Mrs Le Fevres. He was a quiet gentle man, and she made marvellous bread, but complained when Bob hung his socks out of the window! One day I was leaning with my back to the fireplace and my hands on the marble mantelshelf and it came away from the wall and there I was with the thing over my bent back and everyone too surprised to speak – they were just gawping and I was shouting for help!

We decided to look up a friend Bob had worked with in Elliston & Cavells in Oxford. He was away in the services, but we met his sister Margaret and his lovely elderly parents and they offered us a home there. So we moved in and were very happy there. Those days passed in Doncaster quickly; it was a welcome respite and we were sad to leave.

Chapter twenty-three

In October we moved from Doncaster, Finningley to Rugby where Bob was now doing an Instructor's course. Life went on and we were not there long. This was late in the year of 1941 and all women were called either into war work or the services. We asked if husband and wives were posted together 'Yes, if possible' was the answer. So I joined the WAAFS and was posted to Heyford. We were never posted anywhere near to one another, although we managed to meet up sometimes. Bob came to stay in London when he was on leave as I had been posted to Adastral House, London for training and we stayed in the Strand Hotel. We hated being apart.

On Boxing Day 1941, my parents and sister had a serious car accident in which the driver, a close family friend, was killed. I tried to get a release from the Air Force to no avail, however I found out that I was pregnant, was released, and went home to see my parents. I hated being in the WAAFS and far away from everybody. There were aircraft crashes practically every day it seemed.

Bob was posted to Wigtown in January 1942 where he instructed pilots in whatever aircraft they had to fly.

When Bob was posted to RAF Cark in Cartmel in the Lake District in May 1942 I joined him, and it was another lovely respite. I used to walk to the camp and he would cycle back down the lanes with me on the handlebars. We lived with a local nurse and her three sons. The countryside was so beautiful. We met two lasting friends Joan and Tiny, in the RAF too, and we had lots of lovely times together. Ethel, my sister came to stay sometimes and so did Margaret Prentice. I wished my mother and father could have shared this experience, but their car accident had left my mother a permanent invalid and my father quite badly hurt too. Ethel recovered but was badly scarred.

Chapter twenty-four

In September I went back home to live with my long suffering parents because Bob had been posted to Dumfries. Jonathan was born on November 17 1942. He was such a comfort to cuddle and hold. Bob didn't see him for three weeks, as he couldn't leave base. My sister Ethel was a constant visitor at the little nursing home and Jonathan thrived. I believe it was good for my family to share the time with this little boy, though my mother was very frail, and life was pretty tough for everyone. I did try sharing a home with a school friend with children for a time, but returned to my own home when it didn't work out.

When Jonathan was about six months old we joined Bob in Kemble, Cirencester where he had been posted as a Test Pilot. I went trekking around to try and find digs but no-one wanted a baby in the house. Finally Bob found rooms in a lodge to a country estate, by the camp in Kemble village.

We enjoyed the few months there, apart from one night Bob hadn't come home and I felt something awful had happened to him. I packed Jonathan up in the carrycot and I headed off up the drive in the dark to the great house, but on the way bumped into Bob. I've never been so thankful. I remember the constant noise of the planes there. We were with one of our friends one day and he was killed the following week, having taken Bob's place in testing an aircraft.

Chapter twenty-five

In November 1943 Bob was posted to Vancouver, Canada – the parting was unbearable, but Bob was to have an unforgettable experience. He loved Canada and the whole adventure. Jonathan was about eighteen months old when Bob left and they didn't meet up again until he was nearly three years old. I felt sorry for them missing one another, but so glad I had this little boy to love. I went back home again to Mum, Dad and Ethel.

Life went on – Bob sending us food parcels and clothes and writing lots of letters with tales of adventures. He sent presents for Jonathan, and for the family. I waited for letters and wrote endless pages about nothing. I shopped and queued and we got by. My dad made toys for Jonathan. My parents were very good to us, even though they were still fragile from the accident.

We were lucky for there was little major effect from the war in Worcester, except for one day when the Metal Box Factory was bombed. Nearby, Birmingham was getting its fair share though.

On May 26 1945 the war in Europe ended. Bob was still in Canada and I was staying with his mother in Burford, and I danced in the street. Everyone was happy, singing and holding hands with anyone and everyone. I was dreaming of Bob's return, and enjoying myself at the same time. Then the time came for Bob to return home. It was a lovely day. We thought this was the end of flying, but more was to come. He resumed flying again this time bringing back the troops from India and the Middle East. My brother in law was stationed in Israel during the war, and hoped that Bob would fly him home but this wasn't to be. My mother died in 1945 after Bob's safe return.

No

To MRS. R.H. PEARMAN,
173 MALVERN ROAD
WORCESTER.
ENGLAND.

From
F/O R.H. PEARMAN.
(Sender's name)
SPAULDING HOTEL
(Sender's address)
SAN FRANCISCO CALIF.
MARCH 10.
(Date)

[CENSOR'S STAMP]

Hello sweet. The last time I wrote we were
in Los Angeles with very little cash. Yesterday
we hitched up as far as here & are now
trying to contact someone we know well enough
to borrow some cash off. We did about
400 miles yesterday & still have quite a
long way to go. This leave has been fairly
quiet & have been moving most of the time.
Shall be glad when I'm back at Comox
& settled again & then two months & I'll
be with you. I'll have lots to tell you
all about the trip & wish you could have
been here with me. I'm looking forward
to our leave together & seeing old England
again. This country is far too fast for me & one
long rush the whole time.
All my love Bobs

V—MAIL

Chapter twenty-six

In November 1946 Bob was posted to Uxbridge for demob. He was asked if he would like to be flown to Uxbridge for it. He refused saying 'no more flying' and he meant it. He actually didn't fly again until the 1970s when we had a holiday abroad and we had to fly, but I don't think he enjoyed the experience.

Bob's brother John returned home from the Middle East and married my sister Ethel who he had been writing to throughout the war years. He became the headmaster of Hartlebury Grammar School and they had three children.

We settled in Swinbrook, then in Burford, Fulbrook and finally Carterton, the family growing up, and in number.

Bob had a partnership with Mr Paine. They shared the garage on the A40 at Burford for many years – Paine & Pearman.

One day in August 1994 we travelled to Cromer to stay with Jonathan who was teaching there. We settled in at the end of the journey and Bob quietly closed his eyes for his final rest – so peacefully.

I thank God for the great blessings we have shared. What great memories of a brave and good and loving man.

We can never forget the times we lived through, the friends we made and the sacrifice of those who gave their lives.